Passing It On

A Continuing Journey into Honest Horsemanship

Passing It On

A Continuing Journey into Honest Horsemanship

Tom Moates

SPINNING SEVENS
PRESS

ISBN 978-0-9845850-7-6

Designed by Chris Legg

Cover photo by Carol Moates.

Dedication

To my grandson Jake Legg and other young people starting their horsemanship journeys.

SPINNING SEVENS
PRESS

Other Books by Tom Moates

Discovering Natural Horsemanship

Round-Up: A Gathering of Equine Writings

(The Honest Horsemanship Series:)

A Horse's Thought

Between the Reins

Further Along the Trail

Going Somewhere

Contents

(*Pam Talley Stoneburner*)

Foreword

The book you are holding is titled *Passing It On*, the fifth in a series Tom Moates has written. In typical Tom style, he writes of real-life experiences—some his, some others'—and how those experiences bring truth to some horsemanship principles. After many of those experiences, he felt he had enough to offer that he could help others. So, he moved to a new era of teaching others in an attempt to pass it on. You might ask what "it" is. "It" is a way of being and working with horses.

Tom would never claim to have "it" worked out or fully understood, as "it" is a never-ending journey. Along that journey are a lot of folks less experienced than Tom, so Tom feels the desire to help pass along any lessons he can to those a little further back down the horsemanship trail. It's just a new chapter in Tom's journey.

Since he was first introduced to this "better way" with horses, he has been passing it along through his writing. When you put it out there in written form, you rarely get to know how it might impact others and their horses' lives. However, when teaching hands-on, there can be the instant gratification of seeing people change their ways with horses. Probably even more rewarding for a horse lover like Tom is to see the change in a horse, instantly before his eyes.

So, to Tom it probably now feels like he's passing it along when really he has been succeeding at that task in book after book. Again, thank you, Tom, and please don't lose your enthusiasm for passing it on.

Harry Whitney
May 2014

Acknowledgments

Carol Moates always deserves a special thanks when I get to the end of a book. As the wife of this writer, she gets to tolerate months and years of my time being devoted to working on these manuscripts. It also means she takes photos, reads drafts, and gets the pleasure of hearing me talk about horses constantly for weeks on end. Her patience and contributions are greatly appreciated!

As always with this series of books, a huge thank you goes to Harry Whitney. I'm grateful for the life he's chosen to lead, logging hour after hour in his horsemanship clinics to try and convey to folks like me how to improve our relationships with our horses, and how to help our horses relax when we go to work with them. His patient guidance through all my adventures is the main reason for what progress I've accomplished with the equines I've had the pleasure of getting to know. Thanks, Harry!

Thanks to Dr. David Williams for editing this book. Dr. Dave was a college professor of mine many years ago, and I'm delighted he has agreed to again break out the red pen on my work.

Chris Legg's unique graphical design genius has provided the look for this book series, and again he has worked up the layout and cover design. I enjoy the continuity he provides between the titles in this series, and his many hours of devoted work are greatly appreciated. More of Chris's work can be seen at www.bluefinagency.com.

Many thanks go to the photographers whose work provides some visual accompaniment to the adventures in the pages of this book. Ben Henry, Dianne Madden, Pat Madden, Carol Moates, Pam

Tom and Jubal (The Wonder Horse) get interviewed by home school reporter, Olivia Wilkes, during the 2013 Floyd, Virginia clinic.
(*Harry Whitney*)

Talley Stoneburner, and Harry Whitney all allowed me to use their wonderful images. And you'll notice a large number of the photos were taken by Olivia Wilkes from Alabama. Olivia, at fourteen years old, was a whiz with the camera during our 2013 Bible/horsemanship clinic in Floyd, Virginia. Image after image of hers fits just right for illustrating the stories in many of the chapters that follow. Olivia also interviewed me during that clinic for an article she wrote for a homeschooling class which ran in a high school/home school newspaper and then was picked up by America's Horse Daily, the online newsfeed of the AQHA. (I'm happy to report she got an A+ on it.) So, thanks, Olivia!

Chapter 1

(Pam Talley Stoneburner)

First Flagging

The sorrel mare shot backwards 30 feet with tremendous athleticism. She was so quick and so frightened that I barely hung onto the lead rope in my left hand. A flag was in my right hand, and I dashed along with huge strides to stay with her. Taxing my agility to the fullest, I reached out and touched her on the neck with the flag. When the fluttery streamers touched her hide, she relaxed considerably. Only then did I manage to convince her to stop and bring her attention back to me. It was an extreme momentary workout!

The mare stood there for a moment quivering, the flag still touching her neck. I gave her a comforting rub with the flag to which she let down a little more. Then I deftly removed the fluttery insult away from her and placed it behind me, walked up, and stroked her on the nose with my left hand, the lead rope now draped over my left arm. Her nostrils flared in time with her heaving breaths as she recovered from the episode.

Harry works with Loreli, a chestnut Hanoverian owned by Rita and Andy Riddile, at a clinic in Virginia to try and get past her panic of being flagged.
(*Ben Henry*)

"Well now, that was a big reaction!" I commented, a little out of breath myself.

I'd anticipated a sizeable reaction to the flag, which was the only reason I'd been able to hang in there with her. I had hoped, however, to set things up so the initial wave of fear wouldn't overcome her quite as strongly as it did.

Introducing her to the flag for the first time had sparked this little adventure. With her settled down a bit, I went back to introducing it gently as I had at first. I walked backwards while facing the mare and used the lead rope to get her walking towards me as I retreated. Then I slowly brought the flag up between us and presented it to her at muzzle level.

I explained to my new client standing there (and now nearly as wide-eyed as the mare) that if a horse encounters a curiosity in the field she most likely will approach it straight on and inspect it with her nose first. I was working to help her achieve that same reaction with the flag. By having the mare walk towards the flag, I hoped to help bolster her courage by giving the impression that she was on a fact-finding offensive rather than a life-saving flight from the dubious object that was chasing her.

The mare, however, had a similar reaction to it the second time. In an instant, I was back to hanging in there with her for all I was worth as she backed like a maniac. The fierceness of her flight was slightly less strong this time but still was driven with plenty of genuine panic. In such moments with horses it is easy to see how real their concerns can be with humans and/or things in their environment—I mean to say, how life-or-death some of their trepidations truly are in their minds.

Similarly, several horses I've worked with locally in the past couple of years have shown a big, frightful reaction to the flag when introduced to it. To help lessen the fear of a flag for the first introduction, I'll often hold the streamers in my hand to keep them from fluttering. Then I'll present the less active flag to the horse's nose, face, and neck before doing a more active introduction like the kind of approach described above.

Still, even with much preparation to stave off panic when introducing something new and scary, a horse can have a big reaction. Sometimes it's necessary to go right up to the razor's edge with a horse's worry—nearly to the point of total terror—to get her past the kind of panic this mare was experiencing. The thing is, with horses the scary thing must be right there with the horse for a person to prove to her that she needn't be afraid of it. Presenting a spooky object typically is the only way to help show a horse that the object won't hurt her and that she can relax and be okay around it. Every tool we hope to use to improve their peace of mind (rope, flag, slicker, etc.) also must be right there in the moment with them and us to be worked on.

On the other hand, if not handled right, such a lesson can have an opposite effect. A horse can feel justified in summoning up such fear if, for instance, the worrisome thing is removed when the horse is at the height of panic instead of it being removed at a point where ill feelings have diminished. The horse can become certain in her thinking that the fear worked to remove the trouble.

In the case with this mare, I'd decided to introduce the flag because, as with several horses I'd worked with last summer (in 2013), the owner tiptoed around her. Honestly, I found it disturbing that

Harry flags Tinker, a three-year-old Quarter Horse, from the fence at a colt starting clinic in Salome, Arizona in 2014. (*Tom Moates*)

people ride horses, or their kids ride horses (or they and their kids ride horses), that have this kind of extreme reaction of fear and flight when introduced to something like a flag, water bottle, camera, or raincoat. If that kind of volatile terror exists in a horse quite close to the surface when encountering some fairly common things, surely it is of the utmost importance to work towards alleviating it before climbing aboard. Not only will the horse feel a whole lot better inside, the horse and the people will be safer, for sure.

Get some of these things worked out and the horse can be confident and even relaxed when new or strange things approach. Then there's a chance a horse will not hurt herself or someone else when a plastic bag flutters by in the wind on the trail.

At first glance, when I was introduced to this sensitive mare, she seemed to me as though she could be plenty reactive. The owner certainly sensed this on some level and coped with it by avoiding rocking any boats with the beast. The sneaking around seemed to be an unconscious act for the owner who showed surprise when I pointed it out.

In part, I'd been called out to work with this horse to assess her readiness to be ridden on some trails and county roads. I felt that made it my job to point out spots of worry or tension in the horse that concerned me and to provide some ways for the owner to help the horse improve in those areas. Part of what I hoped to achieve in our flagging session was to get the mare feeling better about some

Harry's deliberate arm gesture brings up some worry in Dandy, a gelding owned by Janet Jones, during a six-day intensive clinic in Tennessee in 2014.
(*Tom Moates*)

things, but also to make problem areas more obvious to the owner, especially where rider safety might be at risk.

Pointing out some trouble with this mare required no more than moving around her a little recklessly. When the session started, I abruptly raised a hand when standing near her head. The horse obliged and threw her head in the air, tensed up, and shuffled backwards. I quickly walked forward to her and rubbed her head with my hands until her head came down and she relaxed some.

I repeated my deliberately careless arm gesture followed up by rubbing her to a more relaxed state several times until she let go of much of the concern over my haphazard hand motions. Within a few minutes, she was able to take a quick hand toss in stride and not think twice about it. I thought then that flagging the mare would be a bit of an undertaking but would be quite helpful towards ferreting out trouble in her to work on—sort of a bigger version of what I'd just done with my hands around her head.

Knowing a horse like this is going to have a pretty large reaction to a flag at first really doesn't make it any easier to hang in there with her when the size of the response is huge. It takes some fearlessness and athleticism, since a horse may rear and flee with a panic making her more like a fire breathing dragon than a horse. And, the flagger must have faith that things are about to get better for the horse, even if the horse doesn't know it.

So back to me and this mare...she erupted into a fright and hit reverse so hard that, while I expected a reaction, I was surprised by its intensity. Such panic in a horse is a horrible thing to feel. I've seen it in both Jubal and Festus, among others, and I just hate it. I hung in there with all I had and touched her on the side of the face and rubbed her gently. The touch again made all the difference. I'm always amazed that something so scary to a horse when held at a little distance becomes okay in an eye blink when she finally feels it.

Another part of flagging a horse that I'm working on is the timing—that is, knowing just when it is best to touch the horse with it. I have found this part to be pretty tricky, and I've asked Harry about it multiple times. I've noticed sometimes he dives in and touches a worried horse with the flag and at others he just keeps it close without touching the horse for awhile. It seemed to me that hovering the flag close by just prolonged the worry for the horse.

Harry explained that when introducing the flag, if the horse is terrified as in the example above, he might need to move in quickly and touch her with it a time or two so she starts to understand the

Tom introduces a flag to Stoney straight-on at nose level to start a flagging session. (*Carol Moates*)

Derrick Hicks works with Whisky, a blue roan Quarter Horse gelding owned by his brother, Jeffrey, at a 2012 clinic in Virginia—Whisky is beginning to relax after some flag work. (*Tom Moates*)

flag really won't hurt her. Once that is established and she settles a little, if he approaches the horse with the flag and she is bothered but not completely coming out of her skin, then he will let her work at that awhile. He does so by keeping the flag quite close to her as she moves around—nearly touching her but not quite. Then there will be a moment when she changes and becomes prepared for the flag to touch her.

I'm not going to say this is a simple thing to see or to time correctly. But, I have paid close attention to Harry recently at several clinics when he flagged a horse this way. I've also had the opportunity to play with it on some client horses. I'm seeing what he means.

A horse will stop pulling away in a fleeing panic, at least for a moment, when she realizes that those actions (and thus the feelings that accompany them) don't make the flag go away. At that point, she'll try something different. If the person pays attention, there comes a moment when she turns her thought towards the spooky object instead of fleeing from it. This is one of those situations discussed in some of the books in this series where the person is setting up a search in the horse. When the horse makes that mental change, her head comes down a bit and a tad of relaxation comes into her.

If one waits until the horse arrives at this point before touching her, Harry explained to me, the act has a more profound meaning to her. It's as if she says, "Okay, this being scared stuff isn't working out so well, let me see if I can invite that fluttery bugger in and just have it touch me so I can get this anxiety resolved." If you provide the touch just at the moment when that change of thought occurs, then she feels like she sorted it out, that she invited the flag in and convinced it to touch her. It's amazing!

I didn't get to that point with the mare in the example here. I did stick with her until I could approach her with the flag without her feeling the need to flee. I was able to comfort her by rubbing her with the flag as I would my hand. I also began to put a little more meaning in the use of the flag, like putting a little ask in it to break her stuck thoughts loose and ask her forward.

This particular session sticks in my mind for a few reasons. One is that it is pretty common to see horses ridden that have anxiety bubbling right below the surface. This mare is like many horses, and there are steps we horse owners can take to get them feeling much better inside about specific things that also helps horses feel better in general.

Another point is that many people tiptoe around their horses to attempt not to upset the apple cart and spook them. Actually, it seems that being overly cautious just makes a horse feel as though she is correct in thinking there really is something to fear if her human also is worried by it. It is better to get in there and deal with the scary stuff to prove it doesn't need to be a worry to the horse. This requires we humans go to school on the ways of accomplishing it, which is our responsibility since horses are forced to live in our world and it's not the other way around.

Lastly, even though I pointed out some huge trouble in this horse, I had her feeling better about it before I left, and after I provided the owner some ways to work on it, the owner didn't have me out a second time. Later, the owner expressed she felt that the trust bond between the horse and her had been diminished by the work I did that day.

Perhaps this is the main reason why this example stands out for me. I think "trust" can be confused with "temporarily docile." Of course, trust is of the utmost importance between a person and a horse for a strong connection and a great relationship. It is essential for the with-you-ness I strive to achieve with all the horsemanship I do. But, what is trust really, and how do horses view one another as being trustworthy?

If you've ever seen a lead mare in a herd, you may have noticed she's trusted but not wimpy. In fact, she may be fully prepared to kick another horse's head off. That's not tiptoeing around the others, but the group may trust her judgment to lead them away from danger and trust that if they push things with her, they'll pay the price for it.

I think that the reason I see quite a few horses in the situation this mare found herself in is because people adapt themselves to what they think makes the horse "like them," "trust them," or get "calm." I know from my own experiences—and Niji has been the ultimate teacher of this lesson—that everything can be seemingly tranquil but the horse and person can be in completely different mental places that just happen to overlap and run parallel for a little ways. But the second a person asks the horse to leave her thought and come along this other way...well, that is where the hoof hits the highway and things begin to feel a lot less tranquil.

Sometimes when a horse is moving, positioning a flag near a horse's eyes or poll creates quite a bit of worry—here, Tom addresses that issue with Jubal.
(*Pam Talley Stoneburner*)

The person can be left wondering, "Well, what happened? I thought she trusted me? I thought she liked me?" The truth is, the relationship has remained the same to the horse all along, but without a little "push comes to shove," the truth is never bared for all to see. Better to push and shove a little in the round pen and sort some things out there than practice a policy of avoidance and then discover what happens when some uncontrollable element shows up to do the shoving.

If a horse is unable to readily let go of the thought that something in its proximity is going to harm her, then she can't be with a person at that moment. If the human allows that trend to persist by constantly circumventing any little problematic thing—removing all scary objects from the horse's environment, for instance—then the horse never has the benefit of exercising the act of letting go of those overpowering thoughts. And unless the horse is never ridden outside of only the most controlled environments, what happens when the unexpected happens? You get a wreck.

Harry says, "The best thing we can do for our horses is teach them to let go of a thought." That is exactly the glue that binds all these things together in my mind. If you accommodate a horse's worries, she is never asked to let go of a thought or the anxiety and ill feelings and bad behaviors that go along with it. Get a horse mentally dynamic so that letting go of thoughts, even strong spooky ones, is second nature and then you've at least got a chance of having a horse with you when that truck with a flappy tarp goes whipping by on some county road.

Chapter 2

Rein Switchin' with Jubal Part I: Figuring It Out

Jubal (The Wonder Horse), bless his heart, along with his good qualities has some very deeply engrained worries. But in a setting where the big, sorrel, Quarter Horse gelding can readily keep his mind and body in the same place at the same time—centered right there with me—he is the horse everybody wants. At those moments, he is incredibly handsome, brave, compassionate, a conformational dream, noble, slow to spook, fairly happy to go with the flow of what a person presents, simply saddled, easily ridden, and a big ol' teddy bear of a horse. You really can't help but fall completely in love with Jubal The Wonder Horse!

Jubal and Festus enjoying a late spring evening, May 2014. *(Tom Moates)*

The strong magnetic attraction people experience for Jubal is just one of the many wonders that indeed make him The Wonder Horse. Another of his wonders is how that list of great attributes goes right out the window in the blink of an eye when his mind leaves his body and he becomes a worried wreck. I've covered quite a few of his challenging characteristics over the course of the past few books in this series.

The "safe places" that allow Jubal's mind and feet to find themselves in the same spot at the same time (and thus provide for him to be relaxed and responsive), I thought, were anywhere that Jubal is with his bestest buddy, Festus (The Bestest). But recently I discovered this is not always the case.

Just the other day I rode Jubal and ponied Festus up our farm road and over to a neighbor's place. Jubal remained calm and mentally together at a longer distance from home than usual. It was very encouraging. As we went along, I was working on some things which Harry had shown me (which I'll get to here in a minute) and were making all the difference. Also, I figured having Festus along side us really would seal the deal towards keeping Jubal calm and with me mentally for a lengthy ride.

We crested a hill about a quarter mile beyond where our farm road meets the county road, and that's when I felt it. Jubal stiffened, trembled a bit, and tried to hurry forwards. Even with his bestest bud tracking along right beside us close enough that I could reach over and stroke his face, it was evident that we had crossed the invisible line. Jubal was in the throws of an all-out worry episode.

Drat! Again I remained unsuccessful at keeping The Wonder Horse mentally with me on a ride. This time I was keeping extremely close track of his thoughts, too. At least I thought so, anyway. Before I knew it, his mind had bounced out of his head, was over the fence, and across the pasture to the horizon. The funny thing was that Festus, on the other hand, was hanging out right beside us, slack in his lead line, just as calm as could be—and he's usually the real worrier!

Jubal was having a pretty major meltdown, but within a few minutes of riding (and without dismounting and doing some groundwork, which has been my fallback position so many times at this stage) I coaxed the handsome devil back from the brink of insanity while remaining in the saddle with the best results ever. I used what might accurately be described as a rein-switch/search. My newly discovered help from Harry for Jubal had come during the most recent (2013) Bible/horsemanship clinic in Floyd, Virginia.

Jubal's behavior during the clinic provides a great example of how The Wonder Horse can be at first fabulous and then, in another circumstance, deeply disturbed. On the one hoof, there was Ashley Durbin's situation for which Jubal was perfect. Ashley recently had undergone some very serious back surgery. Her recovery was going quite well, and she wanted to get on a horse again. She'd ridden with Harry in the Floyd clinics for a couple of years and attended Harry's clinics in Tennessee. Trusting Harry, she wanted to have his help to increase her confidence and maximize the likelihood that her first few post-surgery rides would be safe.

Ashley lives in Louisiana. At that point, it wasn't going to be possible for her to trailer a horse from home. We were happy to lend her a horse for the clinic, and Jubal was the obvious choice. He'd be the calm, cool, collected gentleman to work with her in the round pen and then take care of her for those initial rides. Unsurprisingly, he proved to be all that, and her first few rides went flawlessly.

Ashley's travel obligations dictated that she leave the clinic a day before we wrapped up. I'd ridden Niji the first three days that

Ashley Durbin on Jubal during her first post-surgery ride with Harry helping out. (*Olivia Wilkes*)

week and Festus the fourth. We riders decided to have two group
rides the final day which (theoretically) gave me the chance to ride
two horses, one before lunch and one after. I saddled up Jubal for the
morning session figuring I'd ride one of the others in the afternoon.
Little did I know, especially after watching things go so well between
Ashley and The Wonder Horse all week, that I'd be riding the old
boy in both sessions that day working mainly on his unbridled
unsettledness.

That morning, even though Festus was mostly in sight across
a fence and only a little ways from Jubal, my Wonder Horse's worry
switch flipped. He was all apanic in the outdoor arena. Four other
horses and riders and a pack of people watching in the arena did
nothing to distract his worry. All he wanted was to get his body over
to where his mind was (with Festus). Instead of having a lighthearted
ride playing around with half-halts as I had envisioned doing, I had
the perfect opportunity to work on helping Jubal get settled during
one of his fairly frantic episodes with Harry's coaching. It turned out
to be just what I needed to get some long term tools for helping Jubal
with this ongoing issue.

That year in Floyd there were two five-day clinics. I rode in
the second week, and this was the final day of the last clinic. Danielle
Gruber from Tennessee brought her gelding, Cowboy, and rode him
in both weeks. Cowboy could be rather like Jubal at times with the
worry coming up when heading out for tasks and being separated
from his buddies. Over the course of the clinics, I'd observed
Danielle get Cowboy much better about this with Harry's help. By
the end of the second week, she was riding that horse alone all over
the farm with not any trouble in him. Harry had me work similarly

with Jubal there in the outside arena with the group ride going on.

Following Harry's suggestion, I faced Jubal away from his greatest thought magnet—namely Festus—and then walked on. Asking this of him, of course, brought about an attempt to turn and look at, and then hopefully return to, his bestest bud. Harry instructed me to put a little feel on the rein opposite the direction he wanted to turn. This was done with just enough feel to block Jubal from succeeding in getting turned back to Festus but light enough not to demand that he bring his head back the other way. This scenario amounted to an impasse at first, one where Jubal really struggled. Essentially, Harry was having me set up a search with one rein.

Tom works on switching reins with a frustrated Jubal during a group ride in the arena at the 2013 Bible/horsemanship clinic in Floyd, Virginia.
(*Olivia Wilkes*)

The Wonder Horse was pretty stuck and frustrated at first, but I just let him work at that situation. Eventually he hit the magic moment when he decided to let go of the thought of turning that way toward Festus. Naturally, he let go of that thought just to attempt to swing his head, turn around, and reengage it the other way to see if he could get to Festus via the opposite side.

At the very moment when he made the mental switch, the active rein went slack because he stopped pulling against it. I was holding the rein tightly but not pulling on it. Rather, he was pulling against my hand trying to turn his head to Festus. So, it was he who created the tension on the rein. Indeed, he could have let the rein go slack at any moment if he just quit pulling on it.

Next, I quickly and smoothly slid the reins through my hands leaving slack in the formerly tight rein and engaging the opposite rein before he got all the way around to facing Festus. The same situation then played out on that side. It then swung back again the other way, and back again, and so on, and on, and on....

You might ask, if I had to keep repeating this deal over and over and over again until the end of time, what's the point? Well, actually, this brought about considerable focus and relaxation to Jubal after awhile. From the saddle, and from watching Danielle and Cowboy previously, I understood at least some of what Harry was orchestrating with this scenario.

The thing about this little ditty that became so evident to me that morning in the arena was the existence of a split second where, in changing from one side to the other, Jubal actually relaxed. I anticipated it would be in there because Harry had talked about it in regards to Cowboy. Feeling it proved to be profoundly helpful in

Danielle Gruber rides Cowboy past the thought magnet of an open gate while offering on the rein for the gelding to turn back into the round pen.
(*Olivia Wilkes*)

starting to unravel that terrible anxiety within Jubal that comes up when we ride out to do anything.

At one point during the first week of clinic, Harry rode Cowboy in the round pen and opened the gate to act as a thought magnet. Harry showed how the above-mentioned rein search-and-switch deal could help Cowboy start to relax and let go of the very strong thought to go through that gate.

Cowboy proved to be a great example of a hard case at first. The gelding sometimes even bumped into the panels with his shoulders on either side of the gate as Harry took up a rein and blocked him from going through it. Cowboy couldn't just let go of wanting to exit the pen and follow Harry's suggestion, on a rein, to simply turn back away from the gate.

They kept at it. Cowboy let go of his strong thought in one direction just to switch to the other, and then back again. This ability to let go mentally became more easy for him over time. Those small moments of relaxation in there grew, too. It took awhile, but he was becoming a much more relaxed and happy horse for it.

Eventually, Harry was able to circle towards the back of the round pen and head straight to the open gate without so much as a rushed step from Cowboy, at which point they exited the round pen. Danielle was able to get on Cowboy and work on the same thing. Before long she took this little deal out of the round pen and into the arena. By the end of the second week of clinic, they were heading out the gate, down the driveway, and all around the farm. The positive change in Cowboy was huge, and I really enjoyed watching it unfold.

Feeling the changes coming into Jubal during the group ride on that last day gave me the chance to feel what I had only observed with Cowboy. The feel on the reins reminded me of a rusty old metal hinge found in the dirt which is frozen up solid at first. You put some oil on it and at first perhaps beat it with a hammer to get even a tiny bit of movement. As the oil begins lubricating between the parts, it starts to break free and move more easily. Finally, after some effort, it swings freely with just the slightest movement of your hands and is again a healthy, serviceable hinge. Not to say that you should start with a hammer to begin to loosen up your horse's mind (!), but I think the analogy to freeing up a horse's thoughts is a good one—the more Jubal's thoughts let go, the more the joints in his head and neck seemed to lubricate. The net result was much more suppleness in the feel on the reins and a greater range of motion in my horse's body as he relaxed and became more willing.

Cowboy's ultimate protest to letting go of his thought to get
through the open gate with Harry in the round pen was amazing
testimony of just how hard it is for a horse to let go of such things.
While stopped at the gate, not going along with the direction Harry
offered on a rein but fighting it and leaning hard into the panel on
one side of the opening with a shoulder, he stretched one foot out
with everything he had and just barely managed to slip a hoof across
the threshold and out of the round pen. He seemed to put everything
he had into it. That maneuver was just incredible visual evidence
of how important it was to Cowboy to hold onto his thought. It
showed to what lengths he was willing to go to try and get even part
of one hoof to where his thought was (outside the gate) rather than

Danielle Gruber has Cowboy going great as she works on switching reins
with him in the arena during a group ride in late August 2013 at the Floyd,
Virginia clinic. (*Olivia Wilkes*)

be with Harry right there calmly feeling fine in the pen. It made me think what incredible feats must be possible for a horse and rider if we get the thoughts of a horse like Cowboy with-us!

Jubal in the arena during the group ride was every bit as stubborn at attempting to get his body over to his wayward thought as Cowboy had been in the round pen. He was barely holding it together and could hardly hear my requests on the reins, let alone follow them. He found no comfort in the other horses being ridden around him. He was singularly focused on getting back to Festus however he could. It's a terrible feeling to ride a horse that is mentally elsewhere—even Jubal. But, by following Harry's instructions, I was able to bring about those little instants where the gelding dropped his desire to get to Festus on the one side and went to switch to the other. Those miniscule moments were a change of thought, a tiny crack in the fortress of his mind.

In those split second switch-overs, his mind centered right there with his body. His head dropped a touch. There was an ounce of relaxation before he reengaged his original idea (and the worries that went with it) to get down the hill to Festus by trying the other side. By working on this over and over, we stacked up more of those nice moments and provided increasing opportunities to make them stick for longer periods of time.

Then, after working most of the morning, it happened. Jubal actually lined out and took a few relaxed steps straight away from Festus without my needing to do the little ditty on the reins. It was only a handful of willing steps, but they were right in line with where I'd been fishing to go that time, for probably ten minutes. It shocked me at first!

Jubal lining out and taking Tom somewhere. (*Olivia Wilkes*)

Even though straightness and with-you-ness were just what
I was working towards, I wasn't really prepared for the amazing
feeling I experienced when true straightness came into Jubal through
a relaxed and forward thought. It was only for a handful of steps at
first, but what a monumental difference when he let go of all those
other thoughts! Jubal felt available. In that instant it felt like I could
have ridden him anywhere and he'd be right there in my hands.

And then it was over. He returned to embracing his anxieties
and trying to turn back to Festus. Thus we went back to more rein
switching, but I didn't forget the feel of when he lined out for me that
first time.

There was another very interesting point I noticed during this
arena adventure. Before, when I'd ride out somewhere with Jubal and

he'd have a mental meltdown, I'd often try some form or "pressure and release" to improve the situation and get him more with-me. I might make a circle, for example, and up the pressure on the arc towards home and then relax a little on the arc away from home. Most anything I'd try, however, allowed the gelding to inch towards his thought magnet. One of the beauties of pointing the horse away from his thought magnet and engaging only one rein at a time as Harry set me up to do with Jubal is that we actually gained distance away from his desired destination.

When I had Jubal faced away from Festus and he switched sides/reins, it actually inched him away from Festus each time. We typically began this dance near the fence at the end of the arena closest to Festus. By the time I got those nice straight steps in the direction I was asking, we were nearly half way across the arena. We often went off to one side quite a long ways as I held a rein and Jubal pulled against it before he tried the change. I always blocked him turning to the point that he managed to go towards Festus. Thus, when he let go of that thought and swung around to try the other way, that entire turn necessitated his taking some steps away from his buddy.

Typically, anytime a rider insists on movement away from a thought magnet it only intensifies the worry in a horse—sometimes tremendously so. But here, the relaxation that presented in little doses came at exactly the moment when Jubal stepped further away from his buddy. It was shear brilliance, I thought, that Harry was having me set up this search with the reins while at the same time combining relaxation and with-you-ness with the very action (turning and stepping away from Festus) that normally causes greater anxiety and turmoil! Brilliant!

All these things truly are connected. And you can bet it is significant to the horse that relaxation starts to come at a moment when he steps away from his biggest thought magnet. It might take awhile, but if it is possible to begin with then this can become a way of life for the horse, to follow the rider's feel and leave his own thoughts and worries behind.

Much to my delight, although it was quite a lot of work to get there, I ended up with a relaxed Jubal towards the far end of the arena several times that afternoon. The very moment I'd quit with switching the reins, though, he'd realize where he was and quickly get very worked up again. I'd immediately have to go back to work switching the reins or he'd nearly run off with me. But, increasingly, he would just as quickly relax again as I went back to the rein-switch deal.

Jubal shows some relaxation as Tom works on rein switching. (*Olivia Wilkes*)

I spent most of the morning and afternoon group rides that day atop Jubal playing with this. When the clinic was over and the Big-Uns were back home, I rode Jubal almost daily for the next month, including that time we went out with Festus. There were a few surprises over the weeks, like discovering that ponying Festus along for a ride wasn't always a salve for Jubal's worry. But there were good ones, too, as when I decided to ride Jubal through some heavily wooded places on our farm—but that's a whole other chapter....

Chapter 3

(*Olivia Wilkes*)

Rein Switchin' with Jubal
Part II: The Jubal Theory

The rein switching deal Harry introduced me to was proving extremely helpful with defusing Jubal's worry as we ventured forth into the world. Shortly after the clinics in Virginia mentioned in the previous chapter, I brought the Big-Uns back home to our place for about a month to graze off some overgrown areas. I took full advantage of the convenience of having the horses back home and rode one or the other or both nearly every day. I also rode Niji who had lived there all the time. Jubal and I had tons of time to continue working on what we began at the clinic with Harry.

To recap, one big problem with the big sorrel was that Jubal became a worried wreck when I rode him away from home (or away from his good friend Festus). In our post-clinic time together, I began by working him close to home (and near Festus). By my not pushing the envelope and heading too far afield at first, the gelding remained relatively at ease and things went smoothly. Playing around in a safe zone, however, still allowed me plenty of opportunity to see what kind of situations caused the gelding's mind to wander from being with me.

A great example of this occurred when Jubal and I worked in the round pen by our house and I played with using the open gate as a thought magnet as Harry had with Cowboy in the clinic. We experienced very similar results. Riding him around the pen with the gate open, I could see how Jubal's thoughts were sucked right out of the corral through that opening.

Even in the ideal environment of the round pen and with Festus in sight just across the yard, I sensed the gelding's worry coming on. Jubal's brain leaving the pen was all it took for him to get jittery and tight. Granted, the intensity of the episode would have been exponentially larger if we had gone down the driveway a hundred feet, but that was the very crux of the matter. I was seeing more and more how those big problems out there in the world were the same as these little problems in here close to home.

The problem we were having was that Jubal's thought left his body (and thus what was going on right where he was) and focused on wanting to get "over there" somewhere. When I managed to get the brain back in the horse and centered his thoughts there where we were, that's when I discovered a relaxed horse under me, one capable of hearing and following me. It's amazing how basic it sounds, yet I still am learning to see this very thing in more and more (and perhaps smaller and smaller) ways. It just keeps coming back to the horse's thought.

I worked on the rein switching deal in the round pen with Jubal facing away from the gate. It took awhile—at least 30 minutes the first time—to get Jubal to let go of that thought magnet. Finally, the point came where he was more readily letting go of the wayward thought to go through the gate and was turning away from it with a slight ask of either rein.

Next, I worked on facing him towards the open gate from the back of the pen to see if he would walk towards it without rushing. Jubal really kept with me here. He even halted easily just before exiting the gate without that magnetic pull drawing him forward. It is truly amazing to feel the difference between a horse coping with his own desires to get his body somewhere else and a horse liberated from those troubling thoughts and instead centered mentally right there with you.

Just dinking around in the round pen with one rein and then the other, and spending the time it took to get a real change in the gelding each time I used a rein, provided me with such a relaxed-and-together Jubal that I experienced a wave of joy right there (not that Jubal can't have that effect on a person anyway). To feel his now straight steps and an instantaneous response to my requests on the reins was simply delightful. In that microcosmic moment, I felt like I could achieve that kind of togetherness anywhere we went if I just focused my horse work on these considerations: that I focus completely on getting Jubal's thoughts with me, not settle for less than real positive changes to each of my requests, and just carry this round pen experience anywhere we went and duplicated it.

So I tried that. I went up the farm road and he did reasonably well. I circled behind the house which took us out of sight of Festus, and that actually went better with Jubal than with Festus who freaked

Festus and Tom picking pears in the yard after working on some rein switching while riding around the farm at home in Virginia, late October 2013. (*Carol Moates*)

out when Jubal disappeared from view. Then I thought about trying another challenge...I'd ride Jubal in the woods around the place.

The rein switching was working so well at getting Jubal relaxed and with me in traditionally terrible settings that I was feeling it possible to carry it into a dark and tangled wilderness. I assumed it would be quite difficult; we'd be out of sight of Festus and in unfamiliar territory, and there'd be deer, squirrels, and chipmunks lurking (and everybody knows these are horse eating monsters). In short, I expected the greatest challenge to the rein switching test yet... yet I was surprised at the result!

Apprehensive, but doing my very best to seem totally cavalier about it so as to encourage my trusty steed, I rode the Wonder Horse up the road and then cut into the woods. It was a tight squeeze between trees and multi-floral roses where nasty thorns lurked everywhere. I was thinking it would be a bad place for a horse to spook—for both the horse and the rider. Branches stuck out everywhere and already I was leaning this way and that, ducking and pressing through the clutter of it all with brambles and bushes scraping along Jubal and me constantly. Also, branches and trees were down everywhere making the ground an obstacle course of snares to step over. In short, it was a very complicated, claustrophobic environment.

To my amazement, it went perfectly well. In truth, it went way better than when I simply tried to ride Jubal the same distance away from home down the open road. Then it happened...we jumped a small herd of deer. I heard a bunch of crashing around ahead and to the right. Then I saw four white tails scatter from the underbrush and go bouncing out of there.

Jubal never really flinched! He looked over as they left town. I asked him with one rein to mentally leave that bunch of panicked does and go with me back over the other way, and he was right there. I couldn't have been more delighted with the results. It was a stellar example of an adverse condition where our work had really paid off. It also was a relief that I remained safely aboard my big horse rather than wrapped around a branch dangling from a tree.

I then realized I had been thinking about riding in the woods backwards (not considering riding backwards in the woods, but thinking about it backwards...). The difficult conditions of the thickets and the forest, I thought, would make keeping Jubal with me harder, but that was incorrect. The woods presented such a complicated environment to negotiate that it was essential for Jubal to focus right there where his body was to accomplish walking under, around, over, and between all the stuff.

The minefield of wood, bush, vine, deer, and thorn actually aided me in keeping his thoughts right with us in the moment and proximity. Even the deer bolting episode, which probably would have been a good-sized spooking event on the road, provoked little more than a glance from Jubal. All the obstacle-course-like maneuvering was a big help, not a hindrance.

The experience caused me to consider my initial apprehension about entering the woods. Had I simply not given Jubal enough credit that he could ace it? We were going better in ideal conditions, which no-doubt helped when we went into more adverse situations. A large part of my concern, though, was based on the solid evidence of his many prior troubles that occurred when he rounded the bend out of sight of home and his buddy. I figured the woods would be just such a place times five, with all the added trouble lurking there.

Upon reflection, I realized I had missed the point that the complexities of the woods provided a great tool to give Jubal all the more reason to keep his mind centered on what we needed to do in the moment. This proved to be a great asset. It also provided me with a new reason to ride a horse in an obstacle course, like the "playground" set up at Harry's place in Arizona. Of course I knew riding in such places provided challenges so a horse and person could test themselves in various strange situations before being in some serious real world settings. For instance, Harry's place has a wooden bridge, a big teeter totter, a mailbox, a tarp to walk over, tires filled with dirt to step up onto, a pit filled with plastic bottles to walk through, tall logs to step over, and many more fun things. I have taken horses and played with these kind of things to see what spooking or other problems surface.

I always thought of such obstacles as thought magnets which intensify the likelihood of a horse's thought being distracted from the rider to them. Therefore, I used an obstacle as a challenge, one where the horse would be worried and/or curious about what all the new things were. That trip in the woods with Jubal turned my prior concept upside down. Now I realized a playground, woods, or any difficult area where a horse must pay close attention to how he moves around can be a reason for the horse to keep his mind close by. It can be more difficult for the horse to be worried about his buddy over yonder or where he'd rather be heading if he's about to fall off a bridge right here, right now.

To test my theory (I think I shall call it The Jubal Theory), I decided to give the woods a try with Niji. Upon returning from the recent clinic just up the road in Floyd, Virginia, that year, I also had begun using the rein switching deal with him. The results were excellent. If you're familiar with this series of books, you know I have a long history of missing many times when Niji's thoughts are elsewhere, and sometimes to dramatic effect! Some of our struggles stemmed from the fact that when I was in the saddle I just couldn't keep track of when Niji's mind left the scene.

The worst part about this issue was that, to me, things could seem to be going perfectly well, then BAM!, Niji would react big. We'd go from getting along famously (it seemed to me), even out of the round pen and around the place, then suddenly (at least suddenly to

Tom at the round pen during the 2013 Floyd, Virginia clinic where he watched Harry and Danielle Gruber work on rein switching with Cowboy.
(*Olivia Wilkes*)

me, but I bet not to Niji), he would blast into a romping, bucking fit.

I realize now that the gelding likely followed my requests as a secondary thought, at least for awhile. I think his own thoughts held a primary space in his mind at those times. I also believe his desire to follow his own pressing ideas built over time even though he went along with what I asked. Still, the booger just held out for an opportunity to act and get his body over to where his mind was. At some point, something would tip him over the edge and off he would go after those strong thoughts with poor me along for the ride.

The triggers usually seemed to be when we passed near some area of importance to him, like the beginning of a road that lead somewhere he wanted to go. I distinctly remember one incident where we were walking along the edge of our yard (which we had been doing for ten minutes without issue, playing with various things). It was probably the tenth time we approached where this road cut into the woods. I picked up the left rein to bring his thought left away from the direction of the road, and he bolted right, right for the road, and right under a big White Pine tree. I hit a good sized branch, which luckily broke off at the trunk. It came along for the ride until I managed to jettison it 20 feet later, and I managed to hang in the saddle. 100 feet further down the lane I got him stopped, sat there for a second until the adrenaline stopped throbbing in my muscles, and then went back to working with him without any further issues that day.

The other big trigger had been when I asked for an increase in speed. Niji might seem perfectly willing and with me in one area at a walk, but go to the trot and sometimes instantly it was a rodeo. I will say that over time the blasts had diminished in length—I like to think due to the hours of work we put in.

In my earlier horse years, I usually hit the ground when Niji blasted off, and he'd get to wherever he was going riderless. In recent years, however, I've been sticking in the saddle. I can let him blast

Tom riding Niji through the forest testing The Jubal Theory. (*Carol Moates*)

out for a little ways but then keep riding him and supporting him through that moment and through whatever trouble bubbles up in him during it. Then he seems to get it together, his mind and body happily reunited, and we can go about our business without another such episode the rest of the day. I wrote a whole chapter about just such an incident that happened during a clinic years ago with Harry in *Between the Reins* called, "Niji Bolted!"

So I figured, who better to test The Jubal Theory on than Niji? You can imagine how much I didn't want Niji to blast off through the woods! The stakes were high as I headed him up a road and then cut into the thicket of the woods where I'd ridden Jubal while developing the theory. I discovered the very same results. Often I checked in with Niji on one rein or the other. If there was some resistance in the rein, I'd hold out until I got a change in him— his thought came all the way around, his head dropped, and he was with me. Then I'd release and I'd pick up the other rein and see how that one went.

It is difficult to describe the access (the willingness and with-you-ness) I had to both Jubal and Niji in the tight confines of those woods. I wasn't accustomed to having them right there in my hands this way, instantly available to my requests. Even though they both could be just fine to ride in many situations, this sensitivity to my requests was on a whole new level for me.

After riding Niji all through the forest, I went out into the open on a neighbor's place to see what might happen there. We jumped a herd of deer, and Niji acted as Jubal had: he just turned his head and kept an eye on them for a moment as they scampered off. When I asked for him to let go of those critters and take his thought back the other way, he was right there!

I don't think I can do justice to explaining how exciting this whole rein switching deal was for me. With several horses now it has made a huge difference getting them to let go of long time anxiety when being ridden in certain situations. By adding it to the horsemanship skills I already had honed, it really tipped the scale with several horses allowing me finally to ride them into places more safely, and keep them more with me mentally, than ever before.

Again, as happens at times in these books when I share something that was profoundly helpful to me in certain situations, I feel the need to caution the reader and say that this is not a silver bullet that should be applied to every horse in any situation. However, the rein switching deal definitely has revolutionized my ability to calm jittery Jubals when out and about trying to ride and to get something done. Likewise, strong minded Nijis have benefitted, too. It's wonderful to consider that even after years of serious horsemanship study, I'm still learning profoundly helpful insights from Harry and my horses. I'm sure my horses must think so too!

Chapter 4

(*Carol Moates*)

Jake

That autumn (2013) the leaves splashed their splendid
spectrum display along the mountainsides as the days shortened.

Just past the leaf peak, our older daughter, Arika, her husband, Chris, and our grandson, Jake, came in for a weekend visit. Jake was seven at the time. Saturday afternoon, Jake and I stayed home as the others rode up to town to check out an antique shop. No sooner did they leave than I got one of my strong equine impulses.

"Jake...you want to go out and work with Niji some?" I asked.

"Okay," he said.

At a time or two over the years, Jake had sat atop a horse of ours for a pony ride. However, he hadn't had an opportunity to do much with a horse on his own. It struck me that he was maturing and seemed ready to take on some independent horse work.

I'm always ready to grab a horse and to play with something when an opportunity arises. At that time, I was delighted with the results from the recent rein-switching experiences described in the previous chapters. It occurred to me that Niji was going great. I figured that in the round pen he would be a good choice for Jake to enjoy some premier horsemanship experiences.

That morning, it was spitting rain. Regardless of a little drizzle, when the adults departed (leaving us kids) I thought Jake would be as keen as I was to work with Niji. The footing was a little damp in the round pen but not yet slick. The clouds hung low to the ground and it looked like it could really rain at any moment. I grabbed a halter and lead rope, then Jake and I headed out to fetch Niji.

The big bounce in Jake's step revealed his excitement at our adventure. There was a spring in mine, too. Niji met us at the gate. He's a curious sort of horse and is always happy to go adventuring.

I opened the gate and we entered the paddock. Jake immediately walked up to Niji and buried both hands in his thick sorrel winter coat. I showed Jake how to tie a rope halter so the knot won't cinch tight. Then I played with getting Niji's thought with me. Jake paid attention as I got Niji's mind and eyes centered up on me. Then I showed him how to send the gelding's thought over to one direction by gently suggesting with a hand on the lead rope.

"When you go to ask Niji something you need to check first and see that he is mentally with you," I explained, demonstrating the ground work. "Then when you have his attention, ask what you want him to do by offering a feel on the rope. When he does it, you need to stop the asking immediately—that's how he knows he got the right answer."

There's something especially special about passing on what you're passionate about to the next generation. It seems it can affect you as much as it does the youngster. I always enjoy sharing what I've learned from Harry and horses with others, but working with young people is particularly fun. I think about many of the older riders I work with these days and how they often are attempting to reprogram years of not-so-handy horsemanship. What a wonderful opportunity it is when I get to share some of this unique knowledge at the very start of a person's horse experience!

Jake struggled a bit at first. I'd show him how to ask Niji to back, for instance. I'd see if Niji's mind was with me, then I'd put a little feel on the lead rope, he'd start to commit to backing and I'd release and watch his step come through. Then Jake gave it a try. He caught on quickly and smiled wide at this incredible experience of easily communicating with a horse. Jake led Niji as I walked along coaching him when necessary. We stopped outside the door to our mud/tack room. I stepped in, handed out a brush to Jake, and grabbed the saddle and other things we'd need.

Jake brushed the mud off Niji. Next I took plenty of time showing him how the saddle pad fits, how the saddle sets in place atop it, and then how the cinch tightens to properly hold the rig in place. Then we headed for the round pen.

I had Jake climb up and sit on top of a panel while I did more ground work with Niji on line. I talked through the basics of what I was doing so Jake could follow and stressed how important it was for me to have Niji's mind with me each time we went to do anything. When everything was going smoothly I put the bridle on him and stepped up in the saddle. Then I rode around, again demonstrating some basics and doing my best to explain things simply to Jake.

The lad's eyes were big when Niji and I swung up next to him

Jake climbs up on a panel as Tom puts the bridle on Niji. (*Carol Moates*)

by the panel and had him slip over into the saddle in front of me. I asked Niji to walk off, and we rode around like that in the round pen for awhile. This provided Jake the chance to feel the horse move beneath him. It also allowed him to observe up close my hands on the reins as I asked Niji to back or think around to either side while I played a bit.

Before long he seemed to be up to speed on all we'd discussed so I slipped down out of the saddle and Jake had his first opportunity to pilot the horse himself. It was an exciting moment, but one that taxed my abilities as a teacher from the very start. The first thing I found myself up against was how to best teach Jake to ask Niji to step off and walk.

I realized suddenly that this was a huge concern for me as I stood there on the ground looking at a seven-year-old boy whose feet came only about half way down the fenders on the old swell fork saddle. I knew whatever happened next would create formative impressions on him. I wanted to find a means to get the best possible horsemanship conveyed to the lad while having it be effective. And, I was absolutely certain I did not want to have him "kick to go and pull to stop." If he ever rode anywhere else he was sure to get that advice; how could I set things up to make a preemptive strike against my future foes?

"Lift the reins a little and then put a walk in yourself and see if Niji will walk forward with you," I said.

Jake did; Niji didn't.

"Think about wanting him to go forward and bring the energy up in yourself and walk in the saddle and let's see if he'll pick up on that."

I don't know if Jake brought his inner energy up like I meant, but he became extremely exaggerated with his motions in the saddle. This time Niji walked forward.

Hmmm...now I had a little pickle. This had worked without him being shown to kick the horse, but I hadn't meant to get him flopping around like a bass in the bottom of a boat while in the saddle. I needed to refine this, and right away.

"Okay, just back Niji a couple of steps and stop," I suggested.

Jake carefully brought the reins back—earlier we'd discussed not jerking on the reins. Niji went from a pokey forward walk to a back, and when Jake let the reins go down and rest on Niji's neck he stood still.

"Good," I said to the boy who was grinning an ear-to-ear snaggle toothed smile at his new found ability to communicate with a large quadruped. "Now let's try it this way...."

I knew Niji was a little reluctant to go forward and I sure didn't want to get a battle going between those two. I also wanted to find ways to let Jake experience how it is possible for a horse to follow a feel presented by a human—to make a suggestion, light as a feather, for Niji to go in a direction and then experience the gelding bringing his own body along that way. I had a plan.

"Now pick up your reins," I said, "and hold your left hand still but slide your right hand along the right rein so you've got a little pressure asking Niji to think towards that direction."

His little hands fumbled slightly but he got the split reins coordinated and executed the task quite well. Niji's head, however, remained stiffly straight on the end of his neck.

"Now just hold that there and wait," I said. "Wait until he

thinks around to the right and you'll feel the rein slacken. Don't pull on the rein, just hold it firm and you'll know when he brings that thought around."

A second later Niji relaxed, gave a little at the poll, and looked around to the right. The rein went slack.

"That's perfect!" I exclaimed. Jake set the reins down on Niji's neck. "Now this time, do the very same thing except when you feel Niji give to the rein and think around to the right, try walking forward in the saddle again. Don't do all that crazy swinging; just walk so Niji can feel it but not so big that you'd think I'd be able to see it. Okay?"

"Okay," he said, visibly concentrating on the several things he had to keep straight at once.

Jake picked up the reins and slid his right hand out along the right rein. As if on cue Niji obliged, looked to the right, brought his head around that way, and stepped off in that direction. The gelding walked several steps around to the right with Jake before he stalled out.

I was delighted! By asking Niji's thought to come around to the side he managed to break loose Niji's idea of just looking straight ahead and not going. Once his mind freed up, he was available to feel and follow the walk Jake's seven-year-old body presented. It also provided Jake a chance to experience how presenting something for a horse to go with works to get him to follow along without having to drive the horse into motion.

I asked Jake how that felt.

"Man, that was really cool!" He said.

It really was cool, I have to agree. The rain started and didn't

Jake leading Niji back to his paddock after the fun; Tom walks along with them. (*Carol Moates*)

allow us to keep riding that afternoon. We were inside by the warm woodstove drying off before the others returned from town. Jake talked excitedly about the experience into the evening, though, telling his parents and Grandma all about it.

The next morning Jake, Arika, and Chris were set to leave around 10:00 a.m. Jake asked several times if he could ride Niji so they could witness his newly acquired equestrian abilities. It rained less than expected overnight and the footing in the round pen remained safe enough.

"It's okay with me if it's okay with them," I said.

The momentum of his excitement was an unstoppable

avalanche. The parents said yes, and he skipped along as I walked to fetch Niji while the others packed the car.

Jake and I took our time. We haltered Niji, got his thought centered there, and then Jake led him to the mud/tack room. He brushed the gelding and I saddled him. Then we were off to the round pen, now complete with spectators sitting in some outdoor Adirondack chairs just outside the panels.

We did a repeat of the day before. Jake and I tag-teamed some ground work, then he went and sat atop a panel. I mounted up and rode Niji around a little, again coaching the lad about things like putting a feel on the reins and making certain to ask for Niji's thought to come through before releasing a request. Then I rode the gelding up along side the fence and Jake slid over onto the saddle in front of me. Soon, I dismounted and Jake did a superb job of riding, remembering the lessons from the previous day.

The size of his smile said it all—as did the good sized frown when it was time to quit so they could hit the road. Jake was, however, delighted that he got to show his parents and Grandma that he could ride Niji by himself. Before getting in the car to leave, he took care of untacking and brushing Niji, and then returning him to his paddock.

Carol had grabbed her camera during all the fun. As Jake led Niji and as I walked along beside them returning to the paddock, she snapped a shot of us from behind. The moment we reviewed the photos that afternoon, that one immediately stood out.

"Well, there's the cover of your next book!" Carol said.

She was absolutely right...so it is!

Chapter 5

Poking Horses

"I see people all the time want to do things to the horse to change his behavior but not help him center his mind there. I don't want to be his hard spot. Overall, we give the horse so much to get away from rather than present something for them to go with."

~Harry Whitney speaking at a clinic at Mendin' Fences Farm in Rogersville, Tennessee, 30 June 2013.

Now that I've been working with people and their horses around here locally for a few years I've detected some trends. I should point out that so far none of these horse folk have been acquainted with Harry, aside from perhaps reading about his horsemanship in my books. Many of them, however, are familiar with other clinicians, both through books and videos, and sometimes from attending their clinics. The ones who are familiar with clinicians of the "natural horsemanship" persuasion, so far, all have had one thing in common: they drive their horses to do the tasks they ask them to perform.

This is a symptom, I believe, of one key component to the way in which this new clinician-based horsemanship often is taught. That cornerstone is simply the idea of "pressure and release."

One easily observed, very common, example is when a person wants to ask a horse to walk a circle around him and the tail of the lead rope starts twirling in his hand. This act of menacing the horse to "move forward or else" occurs even before the horse is bothered to be asked with a bit of feel on the lead rope to simply "come along forward *with me*." That spinning end of the rope, you can bet, is directed at the horse's hind end. It's purpose is to put pressure on the rump to get the horse to move forward. It stops when the horse steps off in the desired direction (a.k.a. the release). The truth is simply that it is a threat. "Horse, you better move away from this swinging rope or I'll whack your butt!"

Humans have a tendency to want to press on horses to move them around anyway. It's intuitive for the human—push here, the horse goes there. And then this method is reinforced in people's minds and spreads around like a bad strain of the flu because it is touted by many clinicians on TV, video, and in clinics as the primary means of better communication with horses. I've even seen a demonstration where a clinician asked students to imagine a vertical line at a certain spot along the horse's side where one should put pressure either ahead or behind to deliberately drive the horse either forwards or backward. This unfortunately is an accepted mode of operation in natural horsemanship today.

I can see why. It's easy. It's one of those "three steps to the perfect horse" deals. Poke the horse, wait for a change, then stop poking the horse. Now you've got "willing communication" with your horse; congratulations! Or, maybe not.... Maybe he's just fleeing you because he knows he's about to get poked when you're around. How would you like to be around a friend who asked everything of you with a threat? Regardless, the method gets tossed around constantly because it's easy to grasp and it does get results. It can produce an obedient horse, sometimes pretty quickly, and can look like magic when performed in front of an audience whose horses at home have been a troubling mystery.

Harry, however, takes a different stance on how to approach a horse with a request. His is succinctly summed up in the opening quote. If you think about what he's saying, it makes really good sense. "Don't be your horse's hard spot" is a cornerstone to the kind of willing communication he's teaching people to get with horses. I've found it is absolutely essential to explain the idea of presenting something (a feel) for the horse to go with rather than something (driving/poking) to get away from to my horsemanship clients right away. This is necessary if they are going to begin to have improvements in what they're doing with their horses.

Here's an example from some months ago. It went like this....

I showed up for a first session. The fellow was very talkative; thus gleaning information about him and his horse was easy. They were very experienced. He'd won first place in shows of some kind and had been to see and to ride with a plethora of clinicians over many years. It was very important to this man to be as effortless in his horse work as possible. That is to say, he sought the slightest cue to get a result from his horse and hoped one day that such cues could be minimized to little more than him thinking what he wanted his horse to do to get the proper response. The lightness of these cues necessary to get results with the horse was his barometer of "willingness" in the horse.

I liked his thinking in one sense. I wouldn't mind having a telepathic relationship with my horse either. But what I saw when they started working was heading them in the opposite direction. It was absolutely typical of what I'm seeing in folks working hard to build better relationships with horses by seeking the advice of prominent clinicians. It is in fact 100% typical of my dealings with clinician-experienced horse clients to date. This fellow would just lean forward a little and look at the horse's butt and that horse would spin his hind end away from him so fast it was amazing, to which he'd straighten up and smile. Then he'd cock his head to the side, lean a little forward, and wiggle his little finger in front of the horse and she'd immediately back, and he'd stand straight and grin.

It was evident he was very pleased with this deal he had going with the mare. To him it was a soft and willing communication. It was easy on the horse in his mind, and she certainly was very obedient in reacting to his cues. He thought they were getting along famously. I started to wonder why he'd had me come out at all, to tell you the

Tom watches the action in the "playground" during a clinic at Harry's place in Salome, Arizona in October 2013. (*Harry Whitney*)

truth, since he wasn't asking me much but was telling me tons.

So I was able to observe and listen to him for more than half an hour without getting much of a word in edgewise. During that time, I saw a very different picture of their relationship than he did. When he looked at that horse's tail, she definitely spun it pronto away from his glare, but she swished it and penned her ears flat. Same deal when he did the finger wiggle to ask her to back. It seemed obvious to me that the horse felt very pinched up inside about how she was being asked to do these things.

From this experience I captured a lasting mental image of a key factor that trips people up in their relationships with their horses. I clearly saw a person who thinks that just because a horse reacts quickly and with a very slight cue, it means she is willing—that a willing partnership exists. The honest reality standing before me was that the mare did whatever she could to get rid of this guy and his pressure and release. She felt boxed in and hateful about having to endure this game while she was thinking about being somewhere else altogether.

To return to Harry's words above, "I see people all the time want to do things to the horse to change his behavior but not help him center his mind there. I don't want to be his hard spot. Overall we give the horse so much to get away from rather than present something for them to go with." Everything this fellow asked his horse to do was done in a way that insisted the mare had to get away from him. And it wasn't just backing and disengaging the hind end. It was in how he asked her to move forward to circle him, and even how he used his legs when riding to ask for a turn. Driving seemed to be the very baseline of all his interactions with his horse.

I'm not picking on this fellow in particular to be mean. I'm simply using my experience with this anonymous individual to give a real example of what I see every time I go work with a new person who has spent time trying to get a better relationship with a horse by following the suggestions of many horsemanship clinicians out there. In these situations, I see my job as trying to get a change in how the person thinks about and presents an ask of his horse. This requires an altogether change in the person's thinking and approach. Changing the person's fundamental ideas to set this up can be a real trick.

The key is right there in Harry's words. It is two fold: help the horse get his mind here, and once he is mentally present give him a feel to go with, not get away from.

Harry presents Peacham, a horse owned by Sarah Barron from Vermont, a feel to go with during a six-day intensive clinic at Mendin' Fences Farm in Rogersville, Tennessee in May 2014. (*Tom Moates*)

The horse in this example was very snarky about doing anything she was asked to do. I could see she was mentally elsewhere. The result was that she gave only the absolute minimum necessary to get the guy to leave her alone. I found it curious that by trying to get the horse with him to the point they could communicate telepathically, he actually had created a situation that was quite the opposite. That horse couldn't wait to be over with this mess with the human and to be left alone.

What I observed was, when he asked her something, he poked her here or there and expected her to move away from the nagging of the poke. I think their relationship began with actual pokes, and he'd refined the prodding to where no physical contact was necessary to make the poke work much of the time. He used mental pokes made by slight gestures but nonetheless still pokes for her to get away from.

I explained this idea to him. He handed me the lead rope so I could show him what I was talking about. I put a little feel on it to ask the horse to back. She had no idea what that meant. Certainly, this was due in part to the fact that she was unfamiliar with being asked to back with the lead rope. But, it also was a general unfamiliarity with being presented a feel to go with.

At first, getting big enough to get her mentally with me and then to think backwards, or even lean back before taking a step, took an act of congress complete with a filibuster. I could tell the guy was not impressed. He wiggles his finger and she backs, but I have to throw an actual fit to get her to back—you can see his point. And I suppose one could observe a crazed cowboy jumping like a lunatic in front of a horse until she backs as driving the horse backwards, but hear me out on this one....

Four more repetitions and the mare was backing off a little feel on the line. She was quite sensitive, and I thought that might be part of why she had such strong ill feelings about his poking. I think this smart mare would have been quite willing to do the things he asked, but she'd long ago realized it was hopeless. Instead of working with the human, it's like she'd given up and just went through the motions with minimal effort and no interest except to minimize the poking, so why try? Why even be present for that?

The beauty was that after my few fits there, she really began to think back when I asked. The fits weren't meant to drive her back even though I was standing in front of her. Rather they were a big enough intervention to break her mind completely away from

After working for a few minutes with Punalu, a mare owned by Louise Ellingsworth from Montana, at a clinic in Salome, Arizona in November 2011, she begins to back more willingly off a feel on the lead rope.
(*Tom Moates*)

whatever other distractions she had going at the moment and check in with me. Once she was mentally available, she recognized the feel on the lead rope and very quickly backed willingly.

She wasn't backing straight at first, but no longer was there any tail swishing or ear penning, and her eyes were full on me (wondering what this prone-to-fits idiot might do next, I'm sure). Then, with the horse finally mentally available and somewhat willing, the backward motion improved, and it became easier to shape up her body on a line and get her thinking and backing straight. I thought it was a fabulous demonstration, and the fellow, who was quite a thinker, indicated he now saw how things were working between us. He gave it a try and seemed impressed to have his mare back with a little wiggle on the lead rope.

We ran over about half an hour as he became more interested in what I was sharing about getting a horse's mind with you, then sending a thought with a feel, and then having the horse follow that rather than poking and driving the mare into it. It seemed to me we ended on a good note. Then he never had me out to work with him again.

Chapter 6

(Olivia Wilkes)

Stopping on a Circle

Helping folks understand the difference between a horse "going with you" or "getting away from you" can be quite challenging. I admit that may sound somewhat absurd; after all, the ideas of "going with" and "fleeing from" are opposites, right? Horses are big animals, so how can seeing that difference be challenging?

From personal experience (both as a student of horsemanship and also now as a teacher) I can attest to the fact that in many instances it isn't easy for folks to recognize the difference between these opposites. Discerning this distinction is one of those deals that falls into the category often summed up by Harry and quoted in these books, "Until you see it, you can't see it; then when you see it, you wonder how you never saw *that* before!"

Many horse/human scenarios can be used to help illustrate this point. I'll share one here that I find often works well with my horse clients because it is simple to set up and makes it easy to observe when a horse really isn't with you. I picked this idea up from watching Harry play with it while doing groundwork at clinics a few times over the years. It is one of those things that I took home and tried with my horses. It showed me a big fat hole in my own horsemanship that needed to be worked on. It really helped me improve some things, and I've held it dear ever since.

One of the most basic moves in ground work is to have a horse go out on a lead line and circle around a person. Typically, I find new clients already practice circling their horses. This makes it a ready maneuver to ask them to demonstrate during a session. Once a person gets his horse going around him on a circle, the helpful thing to do is ask him to stop the horse out on the circle. In other words, as the horse circles, out of the blue I suggest the person ask the horse to just stop and stand right where he is without turning and facing in towards the person.

What grabbed me about this little deal is that by all standards it should be easy enough to achieve. After all, the person only asked the horse to simply stop walking right there and stand where he is. How hard can that be, right? It is so interesting to me that very few people (including me when I started working on it, as well as some very experienced horse folk I've encountered) can get it done. This is one reason why it is so effective for pointing out a big spot where with-you-ness is missing between people and horses—it makes not-with-you-ness perfectly obvious.

Equally important to exposing a particular problem area is that this simple deal also provides a specific point where work can be done to improve the willingness in the horse to follow along with a person's requests. Perhaps best of all, this example provides a way for folks to discover in a flash from hands-on experience just what is missing between them and their horses. Likewise, it is easily observed

Tom circling Niji in the round pen during the 2013 Floyd, Virginia clinic.
(*Olivia Wilkes*)

when things improve—i.e., the horse steps out there and then stops when asked without turning in or having some other issues.

The crux of what I want to say here has to do with why so many horses that "readily" circle a person aren't really with the person. This is the "with-you" versus "fleeing-from-you" issue mentioned back at the beginning of this chapter and is the key to the riddle of how people can think horses are with them when they really are not.

First, as in the previous chapter, it is helpful to understand that obedience is often mistaken for with-you-ness. Just as the fellow had his horse whipping her hind end away from him when he simply stared at her butt, many horses leap to the task of going out on a circle around their handlers with the slightest cue. That leap, however, isn't a happy one but rather is a conformity with an ill feeling. It is brought about because the horse has been driven into the act of circling. The horse knows if it doesn't hop-to, then the next thing is a spinning rope, dressage whip, flag, or whatever is coming in there in a threatening way to make it happen. The person becomes the horse's hard spot. The horse knows it's going to get more miserable for him if he doesn't go do this thing. So he flees it—thus he flees the person causing it.

Some see a horse snapping into action with the lightest request and say, "Oh my, how that horse is with him! He did so little to get that quick response." But the horse might be saying, "Boy, I'd rather be anywhere than with that guy right now; let me quickly get this over with!" People misinterpret these signs at times. If they have a chance to see and experience the difference, though, then things improve. That's when the "How did I never see *that* before?" moment arrives.

It is extremely common to see folks driving a horse into

circling from the get go. People also tend to move themselves into position behind the horse for the task. For example, if a person is standing with the horse facing him, it is very typical to see him walk a semi-circle around the horse to come in from behind to drive the horse forward onto a circle. Often folks set out with the lead rope tail already spinning or with some other threatening method already engaged before giving the horse a chance to circle without the need of a threat. Offering a feel to go with first isn't even considered. Or, if perhaps the person starts from a leading position close to the horse's shoulder, he takes several backwards steps away from the horse to then get behind to drive the horse forward to begin the circling.

The horse isn't with the person to begin with, so rather than just ask the horse to move himself over into the necessary position to circle, the person finds it easier to move into a position where he then can drive the horse into the maneuver. Actually, it's much easier to be lazy and just stand there and let the horse do all the work of moving while you direct—but not if the horse isn't a willing partner. I'm sure people do this dance to get into position to drive the horse quite unconsciously, too. I can attest to this fact because it often is a massive undertaking to get people to quit backing up and swinging in behind the horse even when they are being coached not to and are right there concentrating on not doing it.

Usually there are one of two responses from the horse when a person attempts to stop him once he is circling. Either the horse doesn't notice the human because he is so busy going around and around the person in circles (the horse is mentally elsewhere and the person has to get drastic to try and stop the horse at all, which can be rather interesting), or he puts the brakes on hard, turns in, and stands facing the person at a military type of attention. The next step is to ask the person to send the horse out again, go three steps, and stop the horse right there where he is on the circle without turning in. I have yet to see a clinician-experienced client who can do this at first. I view this as evidence that many clinicians today teach students to drive their horses into what they are asking of them and don't do anything to get the mind centered with the person first.

The horse simply is not with the person mentally. If he was, then when the person wanted to stop, the horse could and would stop right there too. There'd be no drama. He'd be paying attention to the human to see if he is asked to turn in or stay out there on the circle, or whatever needs to happen next. He'd be available to hear the human's ongoing suggestions and be there taking care of business. There would exist a feel between them, a constant communication wherein the human had the option to ask the horse to stop on the circle or turn in and stop, or whatever.

This is one of those little trouble spots between a person and a horse that increasingly I'm aware have big implications regarding the overall relationship. If you can ask your horse to go out on a circle for three steps and stop right there without turning in and he does it without dancing a jig or fussing, then chances are the horse is with you. At the very least, he's listening to you pretty well at that moment, and you've handled things consistently enough that what you want is clear to him and he's plenty willing to do it. But if you can't get your horse to do that, it means your horse is not with you for even three steps, so how is it going to look when you go and try to do anything more? I can tell you, it'll look like Niji and me going over a ditch and up a bank when I'm trying to ride down the road as I

Harry asks Gus, a gelding owned buy Laura Kniffen, to stop while on a circle around him during a group ride in the arena at the 2013 Floyd, Virginia clinic. (*Olivia Wilkes*)

shared in a chapter a few books back!

After people try this deal and realize they are experiencing difficulty getting a horse stop on a circle without turning in or flipping out, it is wonderful to see how suddenly the realization of what they can't do becomes relevant. Seeing such a big example of where the relationship goes off the rails gives a helpful, obvious difficulty to work on. The beauty is that the conversation then turns to improving things. They gain the desire to figure out how to accomplished this task. It opens people up to learning as it certainly did for me when I was trying it with my horses and couldn't get it done.

The fix for this can manifest itself in many ways. It can be

Gus stops on the circle without turning in to face Harry and gets a "thank you" pat on the shoulder from the clinician. (*Olivia Wilkes*)

quite personalized to the situation; the qualities of the particular person and horse come into play. But within the local sphere of how to go about changing things for the better for a specific horse and person, the one universal, essential thing is that the person must get the horse's thought present there with him first. Then, the next step is to carry that thought along the way when asking the horse to circle. First, just getting the horse to look out and think in the direction he should go is the challenge. Don't bother with getting a step if you can't get the horse to look and send his thought where you'd like him to go. Sending him out to circle mindlessly from the beginning is fruitless, especially if it is an established pattern you want to break.

Next, can one or two steps be achieved with the horse willing and ready to stop right there without turning in or flipping out? If that is accomplished, can four or five steps work out? This also is a great time to consider that if the horse can't do these simple things and stay with you in the most ideal of conditions, it'll be a hopeless task in more adverse situations.

Increasingly as my horsemanship journey continues, I see the different areas I work on with my horses as all part of the same thing. Earlier along this trail, I thought in terms of different pieces. This piece over here, perhaps backing, as one thing, and then this over here, saddling, was a totally different compartment, and so on. I thought I was getting different skill sets to work with each one. Now I realize the underlying truths of better communication with

Ashley Durbin works on sending Stoney's thought in the direction she wants him to circle during the 2012 Floyd, Virginia clinic. (*Carol Moates*)

horses permeate everything I do with them. No matter what I'm doing with a horse, to be successful at having him right there willing and with me I first must ask, "Where is his mind right now? Is it with me? If not, how do I get it here? Once here, how do I get it to go along with me willingly in the direction I'd like to go?"

To get helpful answers, asking helpful questions is key. The above questions are really important for building a better relationship with horses. I've learned it doesn't always matter how you achieve things with a horse (use a flag, halter, rope, bridle—working on line, at liberty...whatever). If you get these questions answered along the way, then you can achieve most anything and the horse will be right there with you.

Chapter 7

(Carol Moates)

Trouble with Chief

It was late May, 2013. I really hadn't worked with Chief very much over the seven years or so he'd been with us. Chief is my wife Carol's Paint stallion. If you think about the Paint in the Hidalgo movie then you've got an accurate image of this flashy sorrel overo fellow. He's in his early 20s now and is showing signs of arthritis and had a shoulder injury before he came to us that acts up sometimes. Chief lives the life of a king with his own pasture, complete with a roomy loafing shed and is rarely ridden these days. I trim him regularly, but when it comes to substantial work with the horses around here I tend to concentrate on my Big-Uns or Niji, or more occasionally Carol's spotty gelding, Stoney.

A few weeks before this particular day, Carol led Chief from his regular abode to a small paddock by the house to let him graze it off. They went along our farm road for about a quarter mile to get there. It occurred to me as Carol led Chief and I drove along behind them in the car that the old boy was a challenge to lead.

Carol was working pretty hard to keep him on track. Chief's head stayed up, his neck braced, he danced around, and he often got wall eyed and called out in a deafening, shrill holler (I suppose to see if other horses might be in the area and would answer). He wasn't impossible for her to handle, or dangerous per se, but it wasn't easy either. His mind was strongly gone to other places and he provided a really good example of not-with-you-ness. Right then, I realized that over the years my mind had been gone to other places too, not having zeroed in on how not-with-you Chief was in general.

That evening, I walked Chief back to his home with similar results. I ruminated on his actions over the next few days. Honestly, I figured with as much horse work as I was doing, both with our other horses and for other folks around the area, I really should work on getting all of our horses going better. A horse with a mind bouncing around like a pinball when someone is trying to lead him was becoming unacceptable to me in general, and here I had a one right at home.

One thing with Chief, I realized as I turned his situation over in my head, was that I never persisted in what I was asking to the point of getting a real solid change in him for the better. I was guilty of doing just enough to get by but never holding out long enough with what I asked to get a true change of thought before releasing and going on to the next thing.

If he was prancing around and his mind was down the hill when being led, I might put a little bump on the line and he'd get a little better so we could go on. Ten steps later he'd be right at it again. I did not insist on a real, lasting change. I resorted to constant maintenance just to get by with him. I'm not sure why this was the case with Chief when I'd become more vigilant with the others—perhaps I knew he was basically retired so I didn't apply myself to get a real and lasting improvement—but whatever the reason, shame on me! And I certainly did find Chief a fascinating individual, so it wasn't for lack of curiosity and challenge.

Ever since that difficult day of leading him down the road, I'd been waiting for the chance to play around with some things uninterrupted and devote myself entirely to whatever unfolded, however long it took. Finally there was a day with no other pressing problems and I had all the time I needed to devote to Chief.

I'd just returned from four days with Harry as he began that year's run of Tennessee clinics at Mendin' Fences Farm. There were plentiful fresh clinic experiences to help clarify how meticulous to be about getting a horse's thought and keeping it with me every single step of the way. In fact, that week Harry worked with a Fell Pony whose habits and actions reminded me of Chief's. Watching those sessions gave extra good insight into how I might approach the stallion.

Tom leading Chief along the farm road. (*Carol Moates*)

I thought a replay of the walk down the farm road would be a great place to start. I led Chief out of his pasture and onto the gravel of the farm road. The next few minutes proved to be the first time I clearly saw how far gone his thoughts truly were. It also was the first time I was determined to do whatever it took, and persist for as long as it took, to get his thoughts with me and get a real change. The experience proved enlightening!

At first, every step or two I'd check in with him by just stopping to see if he would stop with me. He didn't. If he stopped, it usually was several steps past me and I had to get quite boisterous to even get him stopped there. Two big things from Harry came into play here. One was remembering that at the previous week's clinic in Tennessee someone was working on this very thing. She had a horse blow past her when she stopped.

When working on this, she said to Harry that she hadn't specifically asked the horse to stop, so it was partially her fault. To that, Harry replied, "Well yes, but your stopping *is* asking the horse to stop." The point was that a horse definitely notices when a person stops, and if he is with you he should stop too if you want him to.

Horses are so perceptive there is no question they know full well when you are stopping—even if their heads are up in the air and they are looking at a cute little mare across the pasture, it's unlikely they miss that the person leading them has stopped. They may not care, but they are aware of it. It's our job to be important enough to the horses that they care, pay attention, and react accordingly to what we do and ask. So I figured I should be increasingly expectant that Chief could and would rate me on this, so when I stopped he stopped.

The other big thing was the "Harry-flip" (as I call it) in the lead rope. I've never seen this done by anyone else aside from Harry and those he has taught, and it is wonderfully effective. The Harry-flip is a kind of wave put into the lead rope which travels up the line and gives a sudden message to the horse. It's done with a flip of the wrist, sometimes with a little tug back just after for extra effect.

The way Harry puts a hard flip in the rope not only presents a fairly big message, but in the instance where a horse is blowing past you when you've stopped, it ostensibly gives the presentation that the horse ran into the bump in the lead rope himself. When the flip is presented correctly, the horse goes past you and, BOOM!, it hits him, then it's over just that quickly. It's as if he missed the chance to stop and ran into a wall.

After a couple of those, watching you stop and stopping with you becomes ever more important. The horse learns quickly that to miss what you're doing means he'll come into his own pressure and hit that wall again. You and what you are doing becomes very important to the horse. Watching for when you stop and stopping with you becomes very much a part of the horse's operating system, and he won't be mentally far afield from rating what you're doing when it has importance—not because you are going to punish him, but rather because he gets himself into unnecessary trouble when his mind leaves the scene.

Chief got all kinds of upset when I started doing this. His head would shoot up, he'd rear a little, get all crooked, and dance around. He was truly aghast that I interrupted his thought of going. I just hung in there and not only got him stopped with a Harry-flip, but then kept presenting some feel for him to back up until he did. The back was pretty ugly and crooked at first. It required a huge effort on my part to get bigger to the point he'd take a couple backwards steps. But soon, I also added the insistence that he not only back up, but back straight and with some relaxation coming in there, too. It was a job!

I do not exaggerate when I tell you that I spent the whole way to the house working on this nearly a step at a time. The five minute walk took 45 minutes. The last 10 minutes, however, were way better than the first 35. But, I had to be absolutely insistent, consistent, and relentless with myself to get this kind of change with Chief.

It was tough for awhile, but Chief came through nicely once I held myself up to the necessary standards it required to get a clear and lasting change in the stallion. Once he realized I was not going to give in and let things slide even one time (which took half an hour), he let up on the death grip he had on his own agenda. Things got more relaxed with Chief and between us, and by the time we got to the house, I'm not kidding, you'd have thought I was working with a different, much more naturally responsive horse.

Leading Chief back home that evening showed considerable improvement over the earlier trip. The next day, I led Chief along the same route again, and it took maybe 1/3 as much energy on my part to get excellent results. Then, before taking Chief back home that evening, I decided to work him in the round pen for a few minutes and see how that went. Wow...what a deal that turned out to be!

I entered the round pen with a web halter and lead rope and went to the center. Chief was at the gate, mind gone out of the pen. I tossed the halter at his behind. It hit a bulls eye. He jumped a bit, stood, craned his neck to look at me, and then took off to the left on the rail. Then he turned back and went back to the gate with his head out over the top of it.

I made a little noise to see if he would come back to me mentally, which he didn't, so I tossed the halter again. It landed on its mark and this time he jumped to a trot and went a full circle along the panels around me and back to the gate.

The third time I repeated the halter toss at his bum and interrupted that thought of his being elsewhere, I got a reaction I was not anticipating. Now, I've worked Chief in the round pen quite a few times over the years but never with such good and lasting preliminary work as we'd just achieved with the leading back and forth along the farm road. Also I had the benefit at this point of my own feel, timing, insistence, and experience being further along than at those times past.

When I tossed the halter and hit him in the rump again, Chief let loose! He spun and ran around counter clockwise along

Tom working with Chief in the round pen. (*Carol Moates*)

the panels for about a quarter of the pen and then turned to me and reared. I stood there shocked, just watching his undercarriage and wondering what in the world might happen next. Then he spun on his hind end and tore around the round pen full blast in the other direction. He started bucking and breaking wind while galloping. Then in his wildness, he cut the circle in half and would have run over me standing in the middle if I hadn't thrown my arms up and shouted, "Hey!" He wasn't trying to hurt me...in fact I don't believe any of this was directed at me at all, but rather by my consistently interrupting his thought by the gate, years of pent up frustration seemed to suddenly burst forth.

I'd never seen anything close to this out of Chief before, and I've only seen this kind of thing with Harry at a clinic a few times.

I've seen plenty of horses go ripping around when their thoughts get interrupted, but not so drastically out of character as was unfolding around me. This little rodeo event went on and on, at least for three or four minutes, with the stallion just blasting around all over the place and me just standing there watching and occasionally waving my arms to remind him not to run over me. After a few minutes of all-out wildness, and just as suddenly as he had blasted off in the first place, Chief lowered his head, turned in, and walked right up to me and stopped. I just reached right out and petted his forehead.

It was truly amazing!

I decided to let that moment be and go ahead and walk him back up to his house without fooling around in the round corral any further. Leading him back up the farm road was a piece of cake. He was with me the whole way without any fuss whatever. He wasn't tired, or out of breath, but he really seemed to have dumped some baggage back in the pen. I could check in with him in two steps or ten, and always he was right there stopping with me if I stopped walking. I tried to process what I had witnessed and I felt strongly that somehow something big was letting go inside Chief.

The other thing I noticed directly after this experience was a sudden improvement in another deal I'd been working on with Chief. I'd been trying to help him stop having ill feelings when I go up to feed him grain. When it's grain time, he gets all amped up and when he takes that first bite or two he always throws his head around something fierce. The way I'd been working on this was to stand there ready to feed him, but withhold his grain, or even take steps backwards, until he let that mess go. When he relaxed I'd give him the feed.

I'd been partially successful with this. There was improvement but it certainly wasn't cleared up. Again, I wondered if perhaps I wasn't holding out long enough to get a real change? Or perhaps my timing wasn't great because I had trouble reading when a change really occurred? Regardless, I found it really telling that after the round pen deal, the next three times I fed him his grain there was absolutely no amp up or head tossing when he took his first bites. The grain issue simply dissolved by working with Chief on leading better and by doing that little bit of round pen work (explosive though it was).

It's amazing how work in one area can clear out trouble in others. Not every horse is going to come uncorked and let go of so much baggage as Chief did that day, but even now months later he remains noticeably better overall for the work we did that week. Some of the head tossing at grain time has returned, but it never returned to the severity it was before the round pen experience. It seems there has been some lasting positive impact on this particular horse.

Chief now leads much better as well, I'm pleased to report. I'm very careful to be as sharp as possible every time I lead Chief. I'd hate to admit I'm not 100% on the money with my attention, timing, and technique every time I work with every horse, so I won't admit it. I'll just say I'm hyper vigilant with Chief, especially because he's a strong minded kind of horse that doesn't meet you half way with his attention even though he is a good one for going through the motions without giving you your main focus.

Ultimately, Chief really brought home to me the truth that 45 minutes spent clearing something up today saves fussing with a mess every time you go to work with a horse day after day, week after

week, month after month...and how many hours does that add up
to? It can add up to a whole lifetime of mediocre relationships and
handling. And best of all, with a horse like Chief, the result is a horse
feeling a whole lot better about things, even in his regular daily life.

It's remarkable to think we can have such a positive influence
on our horses when things come together and we devote ourselves
to helping them get through to a better place. To think I may
have helped defuse even some of the years of pent up anxiety and
strong unwillingness to let go of wayward thoughts in Chief is very
gratifying. I'm grateful I decided to get into these things with him.
He reminded me to be on the lookout for the unexpected, and I'm
even more eager than before to get in there with horses (even the ones
here!) and find those deep seated trouble spots and try to help get
them cleared out.

Chapter 8

(*Tom Moates*)

The Delay in Me

I really had no idea that there was a big fat delay in me when I went to ride Niji forward. I did, however, recognize a drag in him.

The second week of the Floyd, Virginia, Bible/horsemanship clinic was underway in early September 2013. Niji was my main mount that week partly because the gelding remained a real challenge for me in many ways. This chronic drag in him was one of them.

On Tuesday, the second full day of the clinic, I was in the round pen riding Niji. I was playing with riding him forward and mentioned to Harry the gelding's lack of willingness to go.

"Well...there's a delay in you," he responded, matter of factly.

Hmmm...really? I cogitated on that for a moment, but I must admit I had a really hard time seeing it. How could I be late in asking for forward if I'm sitting up there asking and waiting on Niji to go, I wondered?

I knew enough about Harry Whitney to know that if he said there was a delay in me that there surely was one, but that didn't mean I could see it. No doubt Harry could tell I was surprised at his remark and that I was struggling to grab an understanding of how it could be.

"Get ready," he said, "and when you want to go forward, do something drastic right then and go to the trot."

I sat there translating his words into visual frames in my head. I studied those, doing my best to string them together like a movie to see if I could predict just where this was heading.

"Get the end of your split rein ready in your hand and when you ask for forward, whack yourself in the chaps," he said. "And get big enough to get a trot. But be ready and slap at the exact moment you ask for go, and be trotting."

I considered Harry's suggestions and knew that the chap slap wasn't to drive or frighten the horse so that he fled forward. It was rather to help me immediately get big enough to break loose Niji's thought of not going when I asked him to go. Plenty of drag already was established in him from my previous puny attempts, so I needed to break that pattern.

Tom works on upping his energy and getting Niji to go while Niji ambles along unaffected during the 2013 Floyd, Virginia clinic. (*Olivia Wilkes*)

I prepared myself. With the end of a split rein readied in my right hand and holding the reins where they crossed atop Niji's neck in my left, I sorted out in my mind how it should go. I gave it a try....

The result was a discombobulated mess!

I lifted my left hand a touch and asked the gelding to trot off, but I got way too wild with my legs and body trying hard to up the energy of my request, and thus I flapped around all over the place. Then, to top it off, I didn't get my chap slap accomplished anywhere close to the point where I would begin to flounder around asking for forward. I must have been four seconds late—that's like an hour and a half in horse time!

The first attempt was so comical I just stopped everything, cracked up, leaned forward in the saddle, and hugged Niji around the neck. Sure, it sounds easy enough doesn't it—just go forward big and slap that chap simultaneously, right?

Even though getting started with this proved to be a rather dramatic failure, it simultaneously was a triumph. The success was that I actually perceived the delay in me that Harry was speaking about.

I felt I was up against an incredible dullness in my mental/ physical coordination. There existed a chasm between my thought (accompanied by a half-hearted attempt) to suggest that Niji go and my own actions to seriously get myself and Niji going. This realization came as a flash when I made the first honest attempt at Harry's plan and failed utterly. It was as if the arm attempting to slap that chap with the rein was in thick mud and I couldn't synchronize my appendage to my brain.

So, I set myself up and gave it another go.

The timing was a little better this time, but it felt like an incredible effort was required of me to get the chap slap anywhere near the moment when I would attempt to ask Niji forward. It is hard to explain this conundrum I found myself in. It wasn't physical. It was rather like Harry said, a delay in me. I had a delay—a sort of unconscious unwillingness—that blocked me from asking and expecting the gelding to GO!

The irony is that I thought all along I was asking Niji to get the lead out of his hind parts and go right now! The problem was that my "right now" wasn't really right now at all.

"It's like you're waiting on him to go," Harry described to me as we discussed the situation, "and then you'll catch up and go with him instead of you going first. You're just sitting there like you're in your easy chair waiting to see what's going to take place and then go with it—and that puts delay in it. You're just behind the action. You've got to make a believer out of him that you're serious, and then you've got to be going."

Reflecting on this situation makes me realize now that these days I'm also getting the opposite side of this type of experience. Sometimes I'm seeing problem spots between people and their horses. Then it's me looking for a way to help people see how they are missing something which works against the horse shaping up. For example, I constantly coach people to avoid walking backwards when asking a horse to circle around them on a lead rope. I had this problem at first, too, but now I can see that particular situation a mile away. Again it goes back to that saying of Harry's so often quoted in these books, "until you see it, you can't see it, and then when you see it you wonder how you never saw *that* before!"

So, back in the round pen, I concentrated extra hard and got a few decent consecutive forward ask/chap slaps accomplished. When my timing and intensity improved, Niji obliged with a newfound willingness to go forward with gusto, and immediately. Then Harry said, "Now put the tail of the rein down and just ask him to go forward."

I did.

I nearly tumbled backwards out of the saddle, so unprepared was I for this new first gear he had. Again, I busted out laughing (along with everyone else)—this time at my own surprise at just how ready and willing Niji was to go. I'd traded in a Chevette for a Corvette!

The thing that really struck me at that moment was how my

poor timing and lack of initial intensity had produced a real mental change in Niji that caused the drag in him. I'd been the real problem here.

The fact that I was so unprepared for Niji to really go freely forward after a little work must have meant that at some level I didn't believe the gelding would be any different than before if I asked with less intensity. The pattern was so established in me (and thus between us) that when it did change, I simply was unprepared for it. I was so accustomed to the drag and my peddling him along to get a forward that it just wasn't part of my reality even though it was what I sought.

Tom and Niji riding along a road on the farm. (*Carol Moates*)

Harry's coaching helped me get a real mental change in
Niji—he was now really thinking forward. Once thinking forward
was on the list of options, all I had to do was ask him to go and there
he went! When he wasn't really thinking forward, I could have asked
him to move out all day long and it wasn't going to get rid of that
drag.

This is a lesson that has stuck with me. I now also recognize
such delays in other areas of my horse work. If I can be consistent
with what I ask a horse, whatever it may be, it's a disservice to the
horse if I don't get him through to a mental change at the start. That
puts a distance between us and keeps the horse from feeling the
best he can about me. I'm also now better able to see delays in the
horse work of other folks I work with. Having Harry state what was
obvious to him sure made a huge impact on me!

Chapter 9

(Pat Madden)

Dinky's Little Worry Cup

Mister Dinky the Mule was introduced in the last book,
Going Somewhere, in three chapters known collectively as "The Dinky
Chronicles." Those chapters provide excellent insights into this little
mule's extreme trust troubles and especially into my working towards
improving handling those homicidally untrimable hind feet of his.

The days when I go to work with Dinky are aptly known around here as "Dinky Days."

Without revisiting all the woes spelled out previously, I'll simply say that when tipped over the edge, Dinky blasts away so hard that there's no way to hold him back. Likewise, if a person confined him and pushed the envelope of his ability to tolerate being handled, there's no doubt he'd kick to defend his life (which I have experienced, although never felt full-on) or try to bite (which I've heard about but luckily never witnessed).

I feel certain Dinky possesses no desire to hurt people or even use a good offence as his best defense; I'd have been black and blue head to toe long ago if that was the case. The mule merely displays "bad" behavior when he feels threatened, which admittedly doesn't take much sometimes. For safety's sake during the first few months, I did most of the hands-on work with Dinky when his owners, Pat and Dianne Madden, had me out to work with him.

Part of the progress with Dinky discussed in the previous book had to do with working directly with his hind feet. I'd initially been asked to come out to see if I could get him trimable. I've worked on approaching those hind feet in many ways: with a flag, using a ring rope to try to get him to relax his hind legs when pressure is applied, etc. Also, I've worked a ton on getting his thought with me and then trying to keep it there as we proceed—not easy with this mule who has a tendency to instantly mentally disappear while standing still (literally lock up wide-eyed and withdraw mentally), or disappear physically (as in, "there he goes...good bye Dinky!"). And, he'll do one or the other of those things ten billion times in a row without offering something more helpful to my efforts.

Although Dinky has made tremendous leaps towards shedding the worst of his general anxiety, he remains convinced deep down that things aren't going to be good for him when a human asks very much of him. That chronic distrust still keeps him from letting down readily, but the accumulation of little improvements we've managed over a couple of years now has him so much better than when we started it's amazing.

For example, at first, just my entering a paddock with Dinky was enough for him to run off and break out into a nervous, soaking sweat, even on a cool day. We are light years past that now, and while it still is somewhat of a rare occasion for Dinky to allow me to walk right up and pet him when he's loose, once I have ahold of his lead rope I can keep him relaxed while we do all kinds of basic groundwork. Honestly, by comparison, a lot of horse problems I come across now seem easy after working with Dinky!

Dinky Days continue. One of the challenges I now have with Dinky is that sometimes he seems to regress. At some point during one of our earlier sessions, I was able to get his hind feet trimmed. Then the next time or two I couldn't—it would be just too dangerous for me to approach due to his kicking and/or running off. I'd try something a little different and again, things would go better, and I might even get his hind feet trimmed. The next time I'd go out, that wouldn't work. I've wondered long and hard about that see-sawing progress...what caused such a variation in how things went from one time to the next?

I can't be sure, but perhaps this back-and-forth deal is a mule trait. I haven't worked with enough of those long eared critters to know if I can blame the whole species or not. Maybe, a new approach produced curiosity enough to allow for a "positive change." Then, after a mule experiences something once or twice, he has it figured out and then won't allow the "positive change" to continue. That's just speculation, but it seems to fit what Dinky and I go through sometimes.

So, it's a real challenge with Dinky, not only to figure out ways to help him relax and feel better about people being around him, but to have any progress stick. True, overall, things have greatly improved with Dinky, but what hasn't changed is his hair-trigger that goes off in relation to various parts of his body at different times.

An excellent example of this disheartening reoccurrence happened about a year ago. One of the first big successes we had with

Dinky is great about having his front feet trimmed these days.

(*Dianne Madden*)

Dinky was that he became completely unconcerned about having his front feet picked up and trimmed. It really was one of the points we looked to as a successful milestone of progress in Dinky's training.

Then, seemingly out of the blue, one day Dinky wouldn't let me pick up his front feet. I'd go to pick one up and he'd slam it back down and bolt away. In fact, it was so out of character for him by then that the first time he did it, I wasn't the least bit on guard and he stomped my foot with his hard little hoof and pivoted on it for good measure as he left the scene.

I never figured out exactly why that happened. I didn't get it immediately sorted out that day, either, although I tried. Finally, I just went to working on other things and kept my feet a safer distance from his front hooves.

The next time I went out, he still had that trouble spot, though not as bad. By the following session, it had disappeared. I have no idea specifically what caused that bizarre regression, or exactly what caused it to resolve, but I think it had to do with Dinky's worry cup being too full.

This is another idea of Harry's which I've heard him share at clinics a few times, and it's one of those things I've never heard discussed by anyone else. If a mule's (or horse's) worry cup gets full right close to the brim, then it's easy to have some slosh out. If, on the other hoof, the worry cup is only half full, then quite a bit can get stirred up without any spilling over. For whatever reason (that I may or may not have been responsible for—who knows what goes on in the mind of Dinky?), the mule was extra anxious those days. His worry cup was extra full and it manifested by his not being okay with things he normally took in stride.

I have Dinky to thank for so many lessons. This regression deal has been a great one, causing me to step back and look at the whole mule and see what I can do in general, or perhaps in other specific areas, that can make his worry cup less full. He has been a master at showing me that if I focus too closely on one thing, like picking up the hind feet, then I may never get progress. I may instead need to work elsewhere to alleviate some general anxiety and then work on the hind feet.

Also, with as many downward spirals as Dinky has dished out, I've seen some extreme examples that prove that no matter how bad things may look when working with an equine, you always can start again and get improvements—somewhere, somehow, if you think about things afresh and keep plugging along. Eventually, something clicks and things start to get better.

Tom works to get Dinky more relaxed with people and activity around his hind end while Pat Madden mans the halter rope. (*Dianne Madden*)

Not getting discouraged and my trying some new tactics with Dinky has led to many helpful changes in him. As Dinky got more at ease and responsive, problems still remained, but increasingly I felt it was safe and helpful to get Dinky's owners, Dianne and Pat, more involved hands-on with Dinky during our sessions. At first, I coached Dianne through doing some ground work including flagging him. Then I helped her with leading him in and out of the barn, which had been a pretty dangerous area because of the mule's tendency to panic and blast away from her in those tight quarters. But all during this time, I continued to have pretty serious problems working around Dinky's hind feet.

I may be able to explain it better this way: from the moment I met Dinky he always was supremely protective of his hind end. At first, the only way I could be connected to him with a lead rope was to stand directly in front of him and ask nothing more than for him to take forward steps towards me or for him to stand. That was it or he was out of there. I was unable to move even slightly to one side off center of his straight-ahead gaze without his turning a quick 180 and bolting. In those early days, you could forget coming along one side of his head or neck, or even touching his cheek, neck, or wither.

Fast forward a year, and Dinky could handle having me move from around his head to about half way down the length of his body. The back half of his body, however, was about as bad as ever. I began concentrating more flagging work on his back end and brushing him ever more towards his hind legs. I'd get Dianne to work on this too, and she continued doing so between my trips out.

As I was trying some new ideas to safely move into Dinky's posterior territory, I remembered something that I thought might help. I'd seen Harry work with several horses in clinics over the years that were very anxious about being approached with flags or other scary objects. Harry helped them to let go of that fear by having numerous people with flags around them—he'd choreograph the troops in how exactly to approach and retreat. The timing and arrangement of this activity was critical to its success, and when I'd seen it done, Harry always got improvement.

I call it "the gauntlet," because it usually ends up with two lines of folks with flags and Harry leads the horse down the middle between the two sides. At first, the folks holding their flags may be all the way against the panels of a round pen, or otherwise at a non-threatening distance. Eventually, the flaggers get closer, and finally they touch the horse with their flags. One way Harry is able to dial the pressure up or down on the horse is by how much of a squeeze gets made between the two lines. I've heard others call this deal a "petting party" since hopefully things go well enough that the horse does get petted by everybody with the flags towards the end. It occurred to me that this might be something that could help Dinky get over the extreme fear of having anything or anyone around his back half.

Dianne, Pat, and I were only three people, not the six or eight I'd seen Harry use, but I was thinking it still could have a similar effect. Hopefully, Dinky would get more relaxed about passing between two flags, and eventually we should be able to let them touch his hind end as he passed through.

I started by working Dinky a little bit on line. I tried very hard to get his thoughts with me and to keep them there. Then, I had Dianne and Pat come into the little fenced-in yard where we work Dinky, each holding a flag. I positioned them at the furthest possible spots to begin. I led Dinky between them. They were so wide, he didn't really care. So I had them come in a few steps and tried again—putting them about ten feet away from the mule on each side. The flags were angled in towards Dinky and were still five feet away from the mule. This time he took notice and squirted forward a little as I led him between the couple.

   We repeated that drill until he no longer charged through. Then they closed in to where the flags nearly touched Dinky. Again as we passed between them, about half way through the gauntlet he zipped forward. We repeated the trip back and forth between the flaggers quite a few times until he became confident and he stopped sprinting as his behind passed between them. I also worked until I

Dinky walks through "the gauntlet" with Dianne and Pat Madden holding the flags. Tom handles both the lead rope and the camera. (*Tom Moates*)

could get him to stop mid-way through the gauntlet and be with-me, back a step, etc.

Next, they came in a step closer and allowed the flags to touch Dinky on either side as I led him through. He took the flags perfectly well on the head, neck, and shoulders, but he really blasted out of there when they got to his back half. We worked on this for awhile, and he steadily improved. Eventually, he was able to take the flag from both sides along his whole body without flinching or fleeing. We worked on the gauntlet over several sessions; each time Dinky relaxed more quickly and got better about it.

As Dinky improved from the gauntlet work, I added another approach, which I had learned from Harry, to see about getting further improvement in the mule. I had Pat take a wrap on a fence

Trying to get Dinky more relaxed about having his hind feet picked up, Tom ropes a hind foot, pulls it forward, and handles it. (*Dianne Madden*)

post with the lead rope and hold it from outside the fence. Then, I used a flag to approach Dinky's hind end. I spent some time at first just walking an arc behind him at a distance with the flag and "switching eyes." At first, Dinky made fast and furious changes, swinging himself all the way up against the fence, and then all the way around to the fence with his other side. Eventually, he traveled about half that distance, no longer feeling the need to go and press his side all the way against the fence.

Then, I began touching his butt with the flag from behind. It was a little tricky at first since he was so frightened about it. But, before long I could switch sides from behind him without taking the flag off his rump.

All these things have contributed to progress with Dinky. It is

Dianne and Pat Madden with their beloved mule, Dinky!
(*Tom Moates*)

so difficult to gain his trust, but in the last three Dinky Days I've been able to trim all four feet. That's big progress, and I was never certain I'd see it. While I do still use the lariat to pick up those hind feet before I handle them, once one is off the ground I'm able to just reach right in there and get a hand on it. I still haven't got him okay with having his feet stretched out behind him for a trim, but we're getting closer each time.

It's encouraging to see Dianne and Pat put the necessary effort and resources into helping Dinky. While it has been a long haul, the results are dramatic. Dinky's thimble-sized worry cup has both emptied to a more reasonable level, and I think it may even have grown to goblet size.

Chapter 10

(Carol Moates)

What Trouble with Chief?

The chapters that comprise the books in this series often relate troubles that someone has encountered with horses (usually that someone being me) and the lessons learned from working through them. An earlier chapter in this book called, "Troubles with Chief," is just such a one. The chapter that you're now reading, by contrast, I'm delighted to say, is being penned for the opposite reason. It highlights one of the more triumphant moments in my horsemanship journey.

I guess I should preface this by saying that what I consider a triumph in this instance, many folks may not think is such a big deal—essentially, getting a previously difficult horse to lead over a long distance while remaining soft and responsive in his body and with me mentally. But this is a moment that stood out for me because I saw without a doubt that the direct application of getting and maintaining a horse's thought, setting consistent boundaries, and insisting the horse relax into a change made a profound and lasting impact on the horse. Let me set the scene and show the source of my delight....

Nearly a year had past since I had worked with Chief as discussed in that earlier chapter. The work I accomplished, leading him along the farm road and setting up what turned out to be a rather extraordinary session in the round pen, brought about some really nice breakthroughs at that time. After that bit of intensive work, the stallion spent the rest of the summer, all fall, all winter, and part of the spring living in his home pasture. Roughly eleven months elapsed before Chief was again haltered for any reason other than just being trimmed or dewormed, so he had not been worked with or led any sizable distance in all that time.

Just the other week (late April, 2014), the spring grass had jumped with some nice rains and hot days. I figured I'd better get Chief across the farm and onto these plush areas by the house again to graze them off before they resembled jungles rather than small paddocks. I'd fixed a few of the fences that had been battered by the snow, deer, and other winter elements, and set up a watering trough so all was ready to bring the stallion over for a feast.

The troubles I had experienced when leading Chief the previous year remained clear in my mind. As I prepared to move him across the same road this spring, I began pondering how much tuning-up might be necessary to get him leading nicely again. I figured with half a year off, there could be a little work ahead to get him sailing smoothly again. Honestly, he had been handling great when on halter for his trim sessions. That seemed to me to indicate that he was not going to be nearly as huge a project as the year before.

Chief and Tom hanging out in the stallion's home pasture. (*Carol Moates*)

But I was guessing we'd have to polish our prior work on this first journey of the season across the farm to remove any tarnish that had accumulated during Chief's extended sabbatical.

When I went to fetch the stallion, he was standing contentedly in the shade of his roomy run-in shed that early afternoon. I put the rope halter on him, led him through the gate, and stopped in the gravel area outside of his pasture fence. He stopped beside me, never letting the loop of slack disappear from the lead rope between us. I backed a couple of steps to see what he would do; he backed right along with me. I stepped forward and started walking down the farm road in the direction of the house, and so did he, right in step. An invisible connectedness was tangible between us—a wonderful feeling, one where he seemed to have let go of any other mental magnet and was right there attentive to me and mirroring my movements. It was as if we were dancing. I led and he followed willingly. What really struck me was the complete contentedness and calmness I sensed in him. It was a joy have that easy flowing exchange with the horse.

Chief kept it up, too, and walked the entire ¼ mile distance to the house without ever once getting ahead of or behind me. The loop of slack in the lead rope that draped between us stayed consistent the whole way. I stopped a few times to check in with him and see if he was truly with me, and he obliged by stopping right then. The with-you-ness was there, and every bit as good as it had been a half year earlier.

I'd hate to think I didn't give Chief the benefit of the doubt before heading out that day, but the truth is, I was surprised at the level of awesomeness with which he led in perfect harmony with me. His mind was centered with me every single step, just like we'd worked on the year before. Sure, that was exactly the goal that I had sought to achieve and is what could and should be...but wow, there it was! And the changes all had stuck. I couldn't have asked any more of him. "Triumph" is definitely not too strong a term for how I felt about Chief's success story.

Tom easily leads Chief along side the farm pickup. *(Carol Moates)*

I reflected on Chief's former difficulties. The year before when I'd take a step or two, he would raise his head and brace it. He would call out in a shrill voice to imaginary friends over and over. He would constantly attempt to pass me or crowd me with his shoulders. That had been quite a different dance from the new one—the former looking like a modern one where we the two participants stand close together but in separate orbits making spastic movements (me trying not to get pushed over or stepped on, and him trying to get his body over to wherever his thought was projected). Before, I couldn't even get a single step backwards from him when I asked for one at first. But now, all those "bad" behaviors, which stemmed from his mind being strongly elsewhere rather than following along with me, had evaporated.

I marveled at how a few hours of work spread over a few days seven months previous had made such a profound and lasting difference in Chief. It proved to me without a doubt that a relatively tiny bit of work can bring about a major and lasting change for the positive in a horse. Putting in a few hours of concentration and toil can result in months or years of great results!

It's one thing to hear Harry or others talk about getting such a change in a horse. It's something quite different to accomplish this with a horse myself. There's a real sense of accomplishment to experience when a horse makes a shift, lets go of a bunch of baggage (and other thoughts), and trades that in to follow my lead while feeling quite still inside about it. It's a real zing!

And, to do so with Chief, a horse that had been here on the place for years before I settled down to business and got some real changes in him for the better, felt especially rewarding. Knowing that this strong-minded Paint that Carol and I are responsible for now can relax when being led and is light and willing on the lead rope is a testament to the lessons I've learned from Harry and horses (and at least one mule) over the years.

This experience reaffirmed the importance of clearing out trouble spots in a horse when possible and not putting it off for days, weeks, or years. Not only is it a service to the horse to have him settled, centered, and confident to be with me, but in cases as with Chief, the positive changes also make him safer for anyone else to handle, as well. It's a win-win situation. I'm more keen now than ever after seeing how well Chief led across the farm recently to clear out even the smallest little blips of trouble in a horse when I come upon them.

Chapter 11

Big Easy Brings Me Full Circle

In February of this year (2014), I had the fantastic fortune to attend a special two week colt starting clinic that Harry held at his place in Salome, Arizona. Harry and two of his long time students, Anna Bonnage and Ty Haas, worked with six young horses and got them coming along superbly in their training and started under saddle. There were accommodations for 20 auditors each week and we had a full house of serious horsemanship students. Suffice it to say, the extraordinary clinic experience exceeded all expectations!

Getting a chance to watch Harry provide the early phases of training for a group of young horses is so rare that I'm writing a book based solely on the colt clinic experience. So, I won't go into much detail about it here. One thing that happened during the colt starting, however, I want to include in this book because it surprised me and caused a moment of personal reflection that seems fit to share.

It was a replay of an earlier event, a real déjà vu moment, that brought me back full circle to a formative experience I had at my first Harry Whitney horsemanship clinic eight years earlier. It was a lesson that has made a big difference in how I've worked with horses since and effects how I teach others about horsemanship today.

I first met Harry in early 2006 when I flew out and audited two clinics at his then brand-new facility in Salome. One of the things I vividly remember is that he saddled Big Easy (a horse owned by his girlfriend, Philly, that he occasionally used as a saddle horse), put the gelding in the round pen, and worked him a little before throwing a leg over him to work a clinic horse or two.

I recall the ground work unfolding nicely, and I remember thinking, "Wow...Harry has that horse going great! Big Easy is so relaxed, I can see he's ready to go to work." But, instead of going to work at that point, Harry brought out a lariat. He built a loop while Big Easy was moving around the round pen. Then he made a throw and sent that loop so it lay across the saddle seat, held in place there by the cantle, and hung down around his bum resting along the back

Harry prepares to saddle Big Easy during the February 2014 colt starting clinic in Salome, Arizona. (*Tom Moates*)

of his legs and tail. The horse felt that rope on his backside and took off like a rocket! Then I thought, "Hmmm...I'd have sure missed that spot of anxiety in him. And if Harry's going to rope and work other horses off Big Easy, it's probably a pretty good spot to have cleared out!"

As I write this, just out of curiosity, I'm going to a shelf in my office and pulling out my old clinic journal from those two clinics at Harry's in 2006 to see if I made notes about that first round with Big Easy and the lariat around his rump. I see that not only do I have notes about it, but I actually drew a sketch to show how the rope went around his bum so I wouldn't forget.

My notes explain that when I was writing this particular entry, I was up at 5 a.m. sitting in the Four Bar J on March 28, 2006. The "Four Bar J" is how I referred to the four-horse trailer with living quarters Harry used when he hauled horses with him to his clinics on the road back then. The trailer's previous owner was Harry's friend, Tom Johnson. His ranch brand, Four Bar J, was still painted on the trailer. I'd say, "I'm heading over to the Four Bar J," when I was going to the trailer. Harry got to laughing at me because every time I said that, he had a mental image of me going to a real ranch, not just a trailer.

Anyway, I was sitting at the galley table in the Four Bar J making notes about the previous day. Here's what I wrote about Harry roping Big Easy:

"After some time spent with the flag, Harry got his long rope. He roped Big Easy around the neck which gave him a bit of a panic. Working him by swinging that rope around his neck a time or two and bumping it around along side his body worried Big Easy, but he changed the thoughts about those worries and got him looking calm

The Four Bar J where Tom stayed on his first trip to Harry's place in Arizona in 2006. *(Tom Moates)*

and with all thoughts on Harry. I figured Big Easy was looking really good and things were winding down. Harry even had approached Big Easy's head banging his coils against his chaps and putting some motion in the rope and got him okay with it.

"So then Harry makes a loop and throws it over Big Easy's butt. It caught from the saddle seat around behind his hind legs."

[Here's where I inserted my sketch.]

"Big Easy panicked again and tore circles around the pen. I was surprised that as good as he was going with the flag and rope that there still was a spot so worrisome to him with the rope. It was a real lesson to see how much trouble remained in the horse in a spot, even after so much work. I would have thought he was good, but then if, say, when Harry was ponying a colt off of him and the lead rope got around his butt, that could have been a terrible wreck."

Quite a bit of work went into Harry's demonstration with Big Easy. He put some meaning into the rope as he continued working with the gelding, like asking for forward with a series of bumps on the line, or asking for stop with a steady pull...but that kind of work is a whole other matter. The point here is that seeing this demonstration has helped me understand that there can be worries in a horse that may be easily overlooked, but can show up in a huge way at inopportune moments if not cleared out when you're working in controlled conditions.

This memory often pops to mind when I go to work a horse I'm unfamiliar with. Jubal (The Wonder Horse) for example, like Big Easy, had plenty of experiences with riders, ropes, and rodeos, but he packed around a surprising amount of anxiety about ropes anyway, especially when they are in the proximity of his hind end.

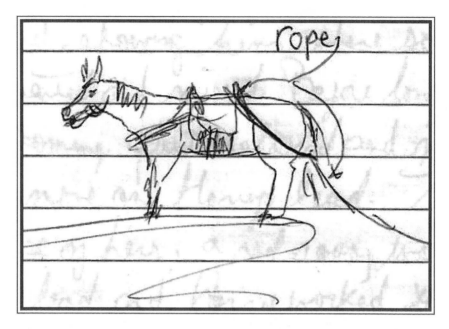

The sketch Tom drew in his journal of Big Easy being roped across his hind end during the author's first Harry Whitney clinic in 2006.

Remembering the session between Harry and Big Easy definitely helped me to be on the lookout for trouble when working with Jubal at first.

The great thing about witnessing this round pen session was that I started to assume far less about the horses I worked with, regardless of how relaxed they might look even after I put in some work with them. I began actively developing the ability to poke around for signs that a horse might have some not-so-obvious ignition points of worry that needed addressing.

The lesson of not assuming that a horse that is calm in many areas will remain so in all circumstances that I took from that early clinic experience has served me extremely well over the years. Such an understanding has helped me ferret out spots in horses (and a certain mule I know) that could have caused wrecks and set back the effort to get them feeling better about things.

In a way this sounds pretty basic, just be sure to check out a horse for all kinds of different worries. But, it's not always so simple to see them. Several years after my first trip to Harry's, I still was missing powerful flashpoints of worry even in my own horses. My horse, Festus (The Bestest), is an excellent example of this.

After being well acquainted with the gelding for at least a couple of years, I was shocked to discover a massive frightened reaction when I was playing with a rope around his hind legs and brought it up above the stifles during a clinic (an incident that is shared in detail in the final chapter of the third book in this series, *Further Along the Trail*). Even though I had worked to find any areas that caused Festus to worry, and there were plenty, I still hadn't gone far enough. I even had worked ropes around his lower legs, for some reason I just hadn't thought to go above the stifles. That lesson with Big Easy from back at my very first Harry clinic popped to mind yet again.

So, fast forward eight years. There I was in exactly the same place at Harry's in Salome, at the very same round pen, and Harry was again in it with Big Easy. This time, I didn't recognize Big Easy when I saw him at first. The Quarter Horse is a stout dapple gray, but over the years since we had last met, Big Easy's hair had turned from a darker gray to almost white. (And...to be honest, mine had undergone a similar transformation!) I asked Harry about the white gelding—once he said, "That's Big Easy," I immediately recognized all of his other features and said, "Oh, sure enough it is!"

On the second day of the colt starting clinic, Tuesday, February 11, 2014, I was perched in my favorite clinic-watching spot,

Harry has roped Big Easy across his back end at the 2014 colt starting clinic——the loop hangs across the saddle seat and drapes behind his rear legs causing him to charge forward. (*Tom Moates*)

atop a round pen panel, camera in hand. Harry saddled Big Easy in the round pen. The gelding was a little flighty at first. Harry did some ground work with him, which settled him down considerably. Then Harry got his lariat, and with Big Easy moving around relaxed and with him, he built a loop and roped the gelding's hind end just as he had eight years earlier with the loop landing across the saddle so it would stay in place on his posterior.

Big Easy bolted forward. Instantly I was transported back eight years to that very first clinic. I balanced there atop the panel remembering vividly the very same scene from my first clinic and felt a curious sense of time as my horsemanship journey flashed full circle back to this place, this incident, this horse, and this clinician—for all I know it may even have been the same rope!

I watched Harry continue to work Big Easy in real-time, but part of my mind wandered, distracted by considering the years since I first witnessed this scenario unfold. I reflected on the horses, clinics, and life events that I'd encountered in all that time. Eight years hardly seemed enough to contain all the amazing experiences this journey has provided me.

After the flashback, my mind returned to the present and put its full attention again on Harry. He now put a foot in a stirrup and stepped up into the saddle on Big Easy. As he rode the big gelding around the round pen, he built a loop and started rather recklessly flopping it around the horse as they walked along. Big Easy seemed fine with the rope banging into him it at this point. Then I saw something I'd never seen before...Harry dropped his loop down behind him and roped one of Big Easy's hind feet as they walked along. Harry kept the gelding walking and lifted that rope up that hind leg as they went. Big Easy might have been a little nervous at first, but Harry handled it so that before long the horse was taking it in stride and walking along completely relaxed again.

My moment of reflection was gone by then, replaced by something that had me fully engaged that I'd never witnessed before—much like watching Harry rope Big Easy's rump had been for me all those years before. The unexpected trip down Memory Trail had been like a mental mile marker on the horsemanship trail that I had traveled.

When I saw Harry repeat what had been such an important moment for me, I marveled that my life had changed course so radically since I first saw Big Easy's butt roped. Between these two similar events, like two covers of a book, the story of my development from a horsemanship novice and fledgling equine freelancer to a relatively capable horseman and full time equestrian journalist and author was written. In that time I had been to more of Harry's clinics around the country than I could readily count. Some horses had come and gone in my life. On the home front, my wife Carol had undergone two liver transplants, which was a real mind boggler in itself. In the midst all of this unfolding, it hadn't occurred to me until fairly recently that somewhere along this trail I'd acquire capabilities enough to teach horsemanship to others.

Sure, I figured my books would help folks by sharing some of my adventures (and misadventures!) and thus pass on some lessons vicariously. But actually teaching others...well, that came about gradually and has been an incredible education in itself. As

Harry is beginning to get Big Easy much more at ease with the rope—here he swings a loop just prior to working a colt with the gelding at the 2014 colt starting clinic. (*Tom Moates*)

with writing about horsemanship, you can't explain to others how to get things going better with a horse unless you have a very clear understanding of it in your own head. Teaching forces the teacher to both ask himself just what the reality is that needs to be conveyed and how to convey it.

I'm still every bit as much a student of Harry's as I was back at that first trip to Salome, and I'm grateful that his depth of knowledge and ability as a teacher continually challenge me. The thing that I never expected is that I'd become handy enough with horses to teach others what I've learned from Harry and from horses along the way. It is a special privilege to understand as much of Harry's teaching as I do, and I'm delighted to help some horses and their folks along my horsemanship journey when I can.

I couldn't have guessed the extent to which my world would be transformed and enhanced by my quest for knowledge about how to get better with horses. Of all God's creatures, the horse has done more to take me down the trail towards truth—wrecks and brilliant achievements alike; the lessons are honest, just like the horses that have tolerated my attempts to improve at horsemanship. I hope I'll get to see Big Easy get his butt roped in Salome again eight years hence, and I can only imagine what parts of the next phase of my life will pop to mind then...!

(Olivia Wilkes)

Afterword

It's a still night at Mendin' Fences Farm in the mountains of Tennessee. It's completely dark now. Frogs and chirping insects are busy vocalizing, and fireflies are flickering a million little yellow specs in the trees all along the wood lines at the edges of the pastures. I'm sitting in a rocking chair on the little concrete porch in front of the screened-in pavilion soaking in the serene scene. Until about an hour ago, the pavilion was bustling with the excitement of supper and the closing discussions that wrapped-up the first ever "intensive format" clinic that Harry had decided to try.

This clinic was something innovative—a six-day clinic with five horses where Harry worked each horse for the first four days and the owners then worked with their horses under Harry's guidance for the final two days. It was a huge success!

Sitting here, I can hear muffled voices punctuated with frequent higher pitched laughter come across the hillside from the bunkhouse telling me that the attendees remain excited about this long week's happenings. Occasionally, from down the hill in the other direction where the horses are stalled, a panel clanks. Otherwise, a solitary feeling envelops me.

I'm rocking alone, laptop in my lap, tapping out this afterword as I reflect on the many times over the years I've been blessed to attend Harry's clinics here only three-and-a-half hours from my home in Virginia. I first came to Mendin' Fences Farm in 2006, just a few months after I went to Arizona and met Harry for the first time. On my first visit here, most of the action took place in an uncovered round pen just fifteen feet from where I now sit. These days, that's been replaced with a roofed arena with open sides—very helpful given the regularity of both blaring sun and afternoon thunderstorms that occur during the May/June season when Harry teaches clinics here.

Sitting here, I realize I've learned more horsemanship lessons than I can count in this little area. Some of my reflections from these Tennessee clinics have been recorded in this book series, although many more remain undocumented. I admit, I am especially fond of

Harry on Jubal in the round pen at Mendin' Fences Farm in 2010.
(*Tom Moates*)

the memories when Jubal came to Mendin' Fences for Harry to use as
his saddle horse for a five-clinic run back in the spring of 2010.

I'm not usually one to be overly optimistic about changes,
especially to well established conventions that I am quite fond
of. But I will say that the special format clinic I just audited was
particularly beneficial for folks, because it allowed attendees to see
Harry work directly with a variety of horses uninterrupted (except for
answering our constant questions, of course) for a solid block of four
days. The relaxation that came into these horses was profound, and
that relaxation became the main focal point of our wrap-up evening
discussion just a few hours ago. That is truly a main drive of Harry's
work—to alleviate anxiety in horses and help people to achieve that

goal with their horses. When a horse lets go of other thoughts, focuses on a person, and the person offers a good option for the horse to go with, then things improve dramatically for the horse and between the horse and human.

Over the past six days, I watched five horses get longer and fluffier as the tension left their bodies. I noticed that during the sessions with Harry, many began to breath and let down in ways that I can't do justice to on this page. I observed all the horses' owners get into the saddle after Harry worked their horses for those first four days and have "wow" moments and describe to us onlookers the difference they felt in their mounts. I understood what they were feeling because I've experienced this kind of moment, too—the most extreme example was when I got on Jubal for the first time after Harry rode him during those Tennessee clinics in 2010.

However, it didn't take long for me to feel that lightness, responsiveness, and with-you-ness start to dull and slip away in Jubal. I'd be much more capable of sustaining some of those wonderful changes today, four years later, than I could back then...but the best of the good still eludes me and slips away. Of course, I'd love to hold onto such beautiful changes in the horses of mine that Harry rides, but I understand why it doesn't happen that way.

That regression happens because Harry is such a gifted horseman, one who has increased his handiness with experiences gathered by devoting his life to working with these amazing creatures and attempting to teach others how to improve their horsemanship. And I'm a student, still some light-years behind him when it comes to horses. Honestly, it just seems fitting that encyclopedias of knowledge remain for Harry to teach me.

I'm happy this is the natural order of things, especially since I've been blessed to have had a horseman as capable as Harry work with me from such an early point in my horsemanship journey. Still, even with those inevitable regressions, feeling that kind of incredible change in your own horse after Harry has worked with him is its own education. In five minutes you feel what can be, and this provides a goal to work towards. You know what is possible with your own horse because you've felt it. That always redoubles my desire to get aspects of horsemanship figured out and going better—because I know for certain what can be.

From left to right: Jamey Wilcox, Ty Haas, Tom, and Harry spend a minute visiting in the rocking chairs in front of the pavilion at Mendin' Fences Farm in Tennessee during a clinic in 2011. (*Harry Whitney*)

Nowadays, I do have breakthroughs with Jubal and the others and recognize the positive changes from having felt them from experiencing post-Harry rides in the past. My guess is Harry's new clinic format will be a repeat venture (indeed, one already is lined up in California for later this year), largely because of the educational value of what cannot be explained, only experienced. Horsemanship must be learned hands-on, not that we humans can't glean great lessons from discussions or books, but when we get right down to it, our interactions with horses are moment-by-moment living exchanges between us and an alien intelligence. That's what makes it so amazing when a breakthrough happens—we've actually communicated with a horse and helped the large, mysterious creature feel the better for it. It's just amazing!

And, as my rocking has slowed to a pitiful pace here tonight and I must get some sleep before leaving pre-dawn in the morning for home, I have to share with you the oddest thing that happened recently. I was working with a client, and I rode her horse for a few minutes to demonstrate a few things that we were discussing about using the reins. I dinked around there on her horse talking while she watched and listened, and then I slid down out of the saddle. She mounted up and rode around, and to my surprise a big grin lit up her face and she exclaimed, "Oh my gosh...he's never listened to me this well before!"

Tom Moates
22 May 2014

(Carol Moates)

About the Author

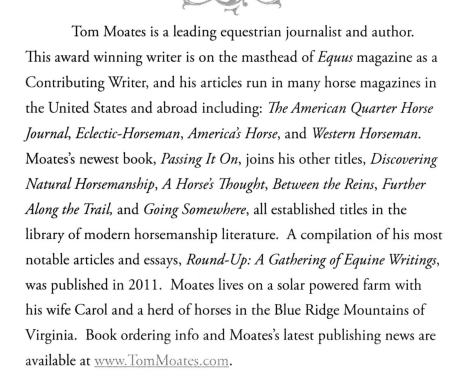

Tom Moates is a leading equestrian journalist and author. This award winning writer is on the masthead of *Equus* magazine as a Contributing Writer, and his articles run in many horse magazines in the United States and abroad including: *The American Quarter Horse Journal*, *Eclectic-Horseman*, *America's Horse*, and *Western Horseman*. Moates's newest book, *Passing It On*, joins his other titles, *Discovering Natural Horsemanship*, *A Horse's Thought*, *Between the Reins*, *Further Along the Trail*, and *Going Somewhere*, all established titles in the library of modern horsemanship literature. A compilation of his most notable articles and essays, *Round-Up: A Gathering of Equine Writings*, was published in 2011. Moates lives on a solar powered farm with his wife Carol and a herd of horses in the Blue Ridge Mountains of Virginia. Book ordering info and Moates's latest publishing news are available at www.TomMoates.com.

CPSIA information can be obtained at www.ICGtesting.com
Printed in the USA
LVOW13s0005030714

392724LV00001B/253/P